Love And Reconciliation

**Insights and Application of
Family Constellations**

By NETRA CHOU

Copyright © 2020 CHOU Tingwen All rights reserved

The characters and events portrayed in this book are fictitious. Any similarity to real persons, living or dead, is coincidental and not intended by the author.

No part of this book may be reproduced, or stored in a retrieval system, or transmitted in any form or by any means, electronic, mechanical, photocopying, recording, or otherwise, without express written permission of the publisher.

ISBN: 9798846748538

Cover design by: Mine Oh

SYSTEMIC AWAKENING
PUBLISHING

Love And Reconciliation

Insights and Application of Family Constellations

Just having love is not enough. The only way to achieve blissful relationships is to take up your correct position and to respect everyone in the family system.

By NETRA CHOU

Dedicated to Bert Hellinger

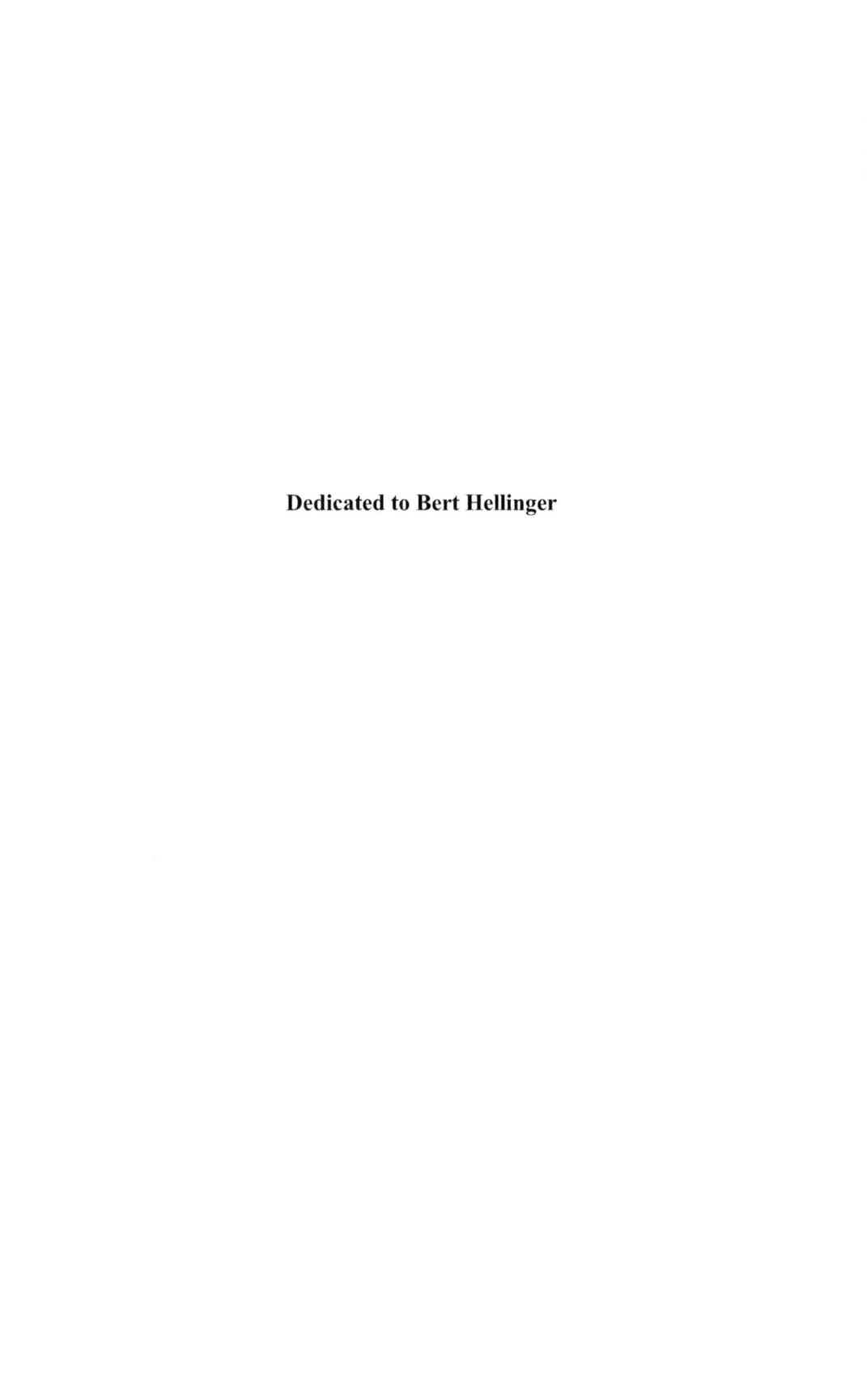

Recommendation from Bert Hellinger

Netra has finished writing a book on the insights and the application of systemic constellation for the masses.

Actually, I had encouraged him to do this many years ago and I am happy that now, even the English version is ready. I feel sure that this book will be of special help to its readers.

It is a special book. I read it in 2 days. It is so close to reality, no wasted words. Everything leads immediately to a solution. And it is a book close to Eastern Wisdom. Above all, it is a book of love, a book promoting peace on many levels, and it is straight forward and down to earth.

Netra has been a pioneer of transmitting the insights and the methods of family constellations to many people, connecting them with the best of Chinese tradition and wisdom. Therefore, I heartily recommend this book. I feel sure that it will assist its readers to resolve many riddles that stand in the way of a fulfilling life, both personally and in their professional success.

Bert Hellinger
Founder of Systemic Constellations

The Author: NETRA CHOU

NETRA CHOU (also known as CHOU Tingwen) born in Taiwan, is a world-renowned Systemic Constellations facilitator. He is the first person to bring the Systemic Constellations method to Asia.

A chairman of the International Asia Conference of System Constellations, Chou has established TAOS Academy of Systemic Constellations in worldwide.

CHOU has been invited to share his work and experiences in various international conferences and has also held countless workshops and internal trainings for various companies and organizations. On top of that, CHOU has also given training in various Taiwanese government agencies, legal organizations, research institutes and even hospitals.

Currently, his workshops are available in Taiwan, China, Hong Kong, Singapore, Malaysia, Japan, Europe and America. Through the use of Systemic Constellations, CHOU has helped many others achieve personal growth and improve their family relationships. In the areas of business and management, he has helped many enterprises resolve their bottleneck issues through the discovery of new and creative solutions.

His bestsellers (Love and Reconciliation; Beyond a Child's Mind; Family Constellation: Core Principles and Training Practices) have sold more than 100,000 copies in Chinese version.

contact:
E-mail:systemicawakening@hotmail.com

Introduction

Through the use of use of detailed descriptions, this book easily explains, in layman's terms, the intricacies and mysteries of relationships and its entanglements. For those seeking love and reconciliation with their partners, this is definitely a useful resource. In addition, the book is a good demonstration of what it means to be "moving with the Tao" and it provides innovative interpretations and examples to go with it.

No one is born to "know it all". It is through imitation and learning that we slowly come to understand something. But to truly master knowledge, it will require thinking deeply through it to derive a more profound understanding and to eventually integrate it as a part of our wisdom.

As saying goes, "When one is lost, one can follow the master. When one is enlightened, one can do it by oneself." (迷時師渡, 悟時自渡) Old Zen masters always encourage their disciples to become independent and flourish as masters is their own right to spread the word and help more people transform bitterness into happiness. CHOU has modeled himself after Hellinger, but he supersedes his mentor with his delicate interpretation of human behavior and examination of the power and esotericism of human relationships. Not only is this the best way he can show gratitude to his teacher, his teachings also provide food for thought in today's fast paced world of fast food culture.

When we have the awareness to watch the path unfold and are given the ability to discover its root cause, we will also find the path of reconciliation which will allow love to flow through it, thus bringing peace to our families and our society.

Xia Hui-wen
Founder of the Taipei Kai-Ping Culinary School

Preface

Having grown up in a Chinese family and having practiced as a Chinese Physician who practices acupuncture, I have had a chance to gain profound understanding about Chinese culture. Since young, I have been taught to be filial to my parents, to respect my elders, to love my siblings, to be loyal to my friends, to be serious and responsible at work. And because I am a doctor, to be ethical in my practice.

In 1997, when I went to Germany to practice medicine and teach acupuncture, I met Bert Hellinger, the founder of Systemic Constellation. That lead to a huge transformation in my life. From a doctor who merely treats physical ailments, I became a holistic healer who supports the growth of one's mind, body and soul through my work as a facilitator and teacher of Systemic Constellations.

Through understanding Systemic Constellation via the experience, I have gained after facilitating thousands of cases, I now have new insights about the typical Chinese family. These experiences have made me aware about the hidden gems and blind spots within the rich heritage of Chinese culture. They have also given me the ability to help Chinese people accept, inherit and promote these cultural gems, while freeing them from the constraints of following the cultural norms blindly, thereby giving them a chance to develop a more matured form of love to live a fulfilling life filled with renewed love and awareness.

These lessons will even be helpful for those who may have grown up in a different cultural background. As the Chinese saying goes, "By other's faults, wise men may correct their own." (他山之石可以攻錯) After we travel overseas or live in a different culture for some time, when we return back to our families or societies, we will find it easier to treasure the good things we have and see the blind spots we may have had. This interaction and stimulation coming from a different set of information and experiences can give one a chance to review what is happening within our families and in our lives and may even become the key to resolving certain dilemmas in life. I am certain that this book will give non-Chinese-speaking families a fresh perspective. Just like how the Tao Te Ching has greatly benefited people in the west, I hope this book will also my readers a new insight into their lives.

As the book is a top-selling Chinese language book about Systemic Constellation (which has been reprinted 33 times), I hope that by translating and sharing these stories from another part of the world, more will come to understand that even this group of different people with yellow skin with jet black hair may be in fact, facing similar challenges as they do. Through these life stories, I hope to inspire more to find the courage to overcome their life challenges. As we realize that we can relate to people of different race who have been living in a radically different part of the world, we will come to understand how all of mankind are actually psychologically interconnected and start to experience how deeply we are connected to one another- We are constantly influencing each other. Regardless of skin color, we are able to empathize and feel each other's emotions. We are constantly running away from pain and seeking happiness and we all share the desire to lead happy lives.

With this understanding, I sincerely hope that mankind will be filled with even more empathy and compassion, resulting in a reduction of unnecessary conflicts and tragedies in our world.

Even though there are many who are familiar with Systemic Constellation and have been facilitating workshops in more than 30 countries around the world, many more may still be unfamiliar with it. Through the sharing about these popular and advanced psychology principals in a book written for easy reading, I hope that it will encourage my readers to understand the principals of life from a different perspective and give them a chance to re-examine their lives, their relationships with their family and family culture while bringing about some positive transformations to their lives.

When I started Systemic Constellation in Asia, the glaring cultural differences between Asian/Chinese and European/American families meant I had to be innovative in my work involving Systemic Constellation. I had to adapt what I learnt to fit with the social and cultural norms of Chinese families. This process inadvertently helped to enrich the Systemic Constellation model. I believe this is the deepest form of respect I can show my teacher, Bert Hellinger- the great founder of Systemic Constellation who is also an ardent philosopher, psychologist and life coach.

Bert has been constantly developing this work of helping others. While working on the philosophies behind this model, he has combined the best of the east and the west. Bert deeply respects Lao Tze and has mentioned that Lao Tze's all-encompassing spirit and moral guideline of "striving to be one's best character just like pure water" (上善若水) is the very essence of Systemic Constellation. This is perhaps why Systemic Constellation is able to transcend all cultural and racial differences to be accepted and well loved by people all over the world. Combining the essence of both Eastern and Western cultures, Systemic Constellation is the bridge that facilitates the "Tao" or the way between heaven and earth that touches the depths within the soul of humanity.

I am really thankful that this book is now published in English as this symbolizes yet another harmonious fusion between the east and the west.

I am deeply grateful to Bert Hellinger for his guidance. He has truly helped to carry forward the wisdom of life. I am also thankful to my translator, Angel Peng, for her diligence and my publishers for all the efforts they have put in. Even though I am listed as the author of this book, the families featured in the book are the ones who used their tears, blood and even lives to give us a chance to learn. I will like to extend my gratitude to every single one of them for their generous sharing.

I believe that the opportunity that made it possible for people to read this book is actually a form of love, and as you enjoy this book, the love will flow on to you:

May those who seek help find help
May those in related professions find sublimation

May the seekers find enlightenment
And may our many future generations benefit from it all

English Version Preface

This is a book about love that does not divide because of race or culture. Every story in the book is an expression of LOVE- the common language of life and reconciliation is the deepest desire of every soul.

Love and reconciliation are constantly happening in our lives regardless of race, skin color or culture. Love and reconciliation is what we are all constantly looking forward to.

This is because mankind shares a common root and this root is none other than our families and homes.

"What is a home?"
"Home is where the heart is, and it is a place built with love."

May this book open the door of love in your heart and bring you home.

NETRA CHOU

CONTENTS

RECOMMENDATION FROM BERT HELLINGER 7
THE AUTHOR: NETRA CHOU 8
INTRODUCTION 9
PREFACE 10
ENGLISH VERSION PREFACE 13
FOREWORD 17
CHAPTER 1: THE DEEPER MYSTERIES OF RELATIONSHIPS 19
    GROWING THROUGH RELATIONSHIPS 20
    UNDERSTANDING SYSTEMIC CONSTELLATIONS 22
    THE 5 PRINCIPLES OF RELATIONSHIPS 30
    REVIEWING YOUR RELATIONSHIP 39
CHAPTER 2: RELATIONSHIPS BETWEEN MEN AND WOMEN 42
    MEN AND WOMEN: DIFFERENT, YET COMPLIMENTARY PARTS OF A WHOLE 43
    RESPECTING SEQUENCE, BALANCING THE TWO SEXES 45
    ABOUT EXTRAMARITAL AFFAIRS 56
    THE DEEP FEAR OF ABANDONMENT 57
    RECOGNITION AND FORGIVENESS OF AN EXTRAMARITAL AFFAIR 58
    THE FLUID PRINCIPLE OF BALANCE 59
    REVENGE AND RECONCILIATION 62
    EXERCISE: APPLYING THE PRINCIPLE OF BALANCE IN A RELATIONSHIP ... 63
    THE EFFECT OF ABORTION ON BOTH PARTNERS 70
    HOW SHOULD PARTNERS FACE ABORTION 71
    THE EFFECT OF ABORTION ON MEN 73
    THE EFFECT OF ABORTION ON OUR CHILDREN 74
    HOW TO COMMUNICATE WITH YOUR OTHER HALF 75
    INNER CONSTELLATIONS EXERCISE: PRAYING FOR YOUR ABORTED CHILD 76
    CONSCIENCE AND THE LOYALTY OF LOVE 83
    PRINCIPLE OF THE FLOW: LINKING UP WITH THE MALE AND FEMALE ENERGY OF OUR ANCESTORS 84

INNER CONSTELLATIONS EXERCISE: LINKING UP WITH THE SOURCE OF LIFE 85

CHAPTER 3: RELATIONSHIP WITH OUR PARENTS 88

LIFE: THE MOST PRECIOUS GIFT 89
FAT WOMEN EAT UP THEIR MOTHERS..105
PRINCIPLE OF ORDER: RETURNING TO YOUR POSITION IN THE RIGHT ORDER TO LOVE 106
INNER CONSTELLATION EXERCISE: RECONCILIATION WITH YOUR MOTHER 108
TRANSFORMATION OF FAMILY VIOLENCE 117
GOING AGAINST THE PRINCIPLE OF ORDER: THE REASON MEN DESIRE INCEST 118
INNER CONSTELLATION: TRIBUTE TO LIFE...119

CHAPTER 4: PARENT AND CHILD RELATIONSHIPS....................................122

CHILDREN: THE MIRROR OF THE FAMILY 123
HOW SYSTEMIC CONSTELLATIONS CAN HELP OUR CHILDREN.............................125
THE PRINCIPLE OF WHOLENESS: DIVORCED COUPLE, UNITED AS PARENTS 131
LETTING GO OF THE PAST AND SELF RECONCILIATION 139
THE PRINCIPLE OF REALITY: PLEASE DO NOT DENY THE IDENTITY OF A CHILD'S PARENTS 139
EXERCISE: PRAISING YOUR CHILD IN AREAS WHERE HE IS LIKE YOUR OTHER HALF ...143
CHILDREN INHERIT ALL UNFINISHED BUSINESS AND EMOTIONS IN THE FAMILY 148
PRINCIPLE OF FLOW: FACING FAMILY PAIN...149
INNER CONSTELLATION: BLESSINGS FOR FAMILY MEMBERS WHO HAVE SUDDENLY PASSED ON 151
PRINCIPLE OF WHOLENESS AND ORDER: UNRAVELING ENTANGLEMENTS................158
WHO BELONGS TO MY FAMILY SYSTEM 161
HOMEWORK: RETURNING TO YOUR ROOTS, DRAWING YOUR FAMILY SYSTEM CHART 162

CHAPTER 5: SIBLING & OTHER FAMILY RELATIONSHIPS 166

FAMILY: A COMMON DESTINY..167
DISORDER CREATES DISTANCE AMONGST SIBLINGS..173
THE EFFECT OF LOSING YOUR SIBLINGS 174
THE EFFECT OF THE FORMER PARTNERS (THE EXES, EX-HUSBANDS, EX WIVES AND EX PARTNERS) 175
LOSS AS A RESULT OF ILL GOTTEN GAINS 181
MONETARY PRINCIPLE OF BALANCE: IN ADDITION TO A WIN-WIN SITUATION, GIVE A LITTLE MORE..183
NON BLOOD RELATIONS: PEOPLE WHO ARE LINKED TO OUR FATES 188
PRINCIPLE OF WHOLENESS: MOVING BEYOND VICTIM AND PERPETRATOR 191

    Homework: Completing Your Family Systems Chart 193
    Inner Constellation: Harmony Begins in The Soul 196

CHAPTER 6: RELATIONSHIP BETWEEN BODY AND MIND 199

    Connections of Mental, Physical And Family: 200
    A Whole System View 200
    Principle Of Flow: Transform The Attitude Of Compensation 206
    Inner Constellation: Listening To Messages From Your Body 206
    Principle Of Wholeness: Re-acknowledging The "People Who Were Excluded" 212
    Undertaking Feelings 214
    Principle Of Flow: Living On Happily 222
    Individual Constellations: Respect Your Family History And Move Towards A Brighter Future 223

CHAPTER 7: APPLYING PRINCIPLES OF RELATIONSHIPS 226

    The Deeper Mysteries of Relationships: Great Love Bringing To Completion 227
    Starting To Apply Principles of Relationships 228
    Develop An Awareness For Your Love, Take Action Now 230
    Table For Reviewing Your Family Relationships 230
    Transforming Into Actual Actions 234

ENDING: AWAKEN YOUR INNER STRENGTHS 236

    Exercise: Taking Action Within 48 Hours 239

[SPECIAL EDITION] BY OTHER'S FAULTS, WISE MEN MAY CORRECT THEIR OWN-UNDERSTANDING CHINESE FAMILIES 240

REFERENCE 248

[APPENDIX 1] TAOS ACADEMY OF SYSTEMIC CONSTELLATIONS 252

[APPENDIX 2] REQUIRED PREPARATION BEFORE ANY SYSTEMIC CONSTELLATIONS PROCESS 253

[APPENDIX 3] NETRA CHOU PUBLICATIONS 254

Foreword

How do we love?

How do we achieve happiness and success? Is there some formula we could follow?

This will be the main topic we will discuss in this book.

The Principles of Relationships.

Do you know what the Principles of Relationships are?

Principles of Relationships refer to the principles that govern love, happiness and success. These are also principles governing life.

However, the mysteries behind Principles of Relationships are often implicit rather than explicit. Only a few enlightened and truly wise souls will understand it or perhaps, some poor, suffering soul might also let out a "sigh" of understanding at the end of their struggle. Most people searching for happiness have failed in their relationships because they have gone against these basic principles. On the other hand, many who have challenges in their relationships get to turn their life around when they understand and apply these principles. The "Principles of Relationships" that we will introduce in this book is the core of the model that is being used internationally in Systemic Constellations. It is the essence and wisdom of many great men and is knowledge uncovered through the experiences, life, tears and blood of countless families and individuals.

In this book, we have chosen to zoom in and analyze our relationships with the people closest to us- our family. These include relationships between husband and wife, parent and child relationships, sibling relationships and common themes surrounding the relationship between our body and mind. The real-life examples I have used in the book (the names have been changed to protect their privacy) come from people who have attended my Systemic Constellations workshops. They are stories that we often come across in our everyday lives and hopefully, they will resonate with you as you enjoy this book. In addition, I have designed and included some simple, yet profound exercises which are greatly effective and can be easily applied to our lives. The content that we have illustrated here has already been used to help countless families all over the world. If we use our hearts to truly understand these concepts and apply them in our lives keeping the faith and move towards love, I am sure life will bring you to another opened door leading to happiness and success!

Chapter 1: The Deeper Mysteries Of Relationships

If your relationships are not deep enough, you cannot fully understand and support each other, you probably will not make much progress in your spiritual practice. If one is lacking in the foundation of relationships and only chasing after enlightenment, meditation becomes an excuse for avoiding relationships.

    --J. Krishnamurti

Growing Through Relationships

Relationships are the best dojo (practice arena) and they present the most rigorous trials.

Relationships, helps us learn, grow and brings us happiness. But relationships also give us challenges and bring us disappointment and insufferable pain. People who live their lives avoiding relationships will surely lead monotonous, constricted lives. Becoming old is not the only requisite of life. In life, we are also required to grow and it is "relationships" that will bring about the most intense leap in growth through the toughest life challenges.

John Donne said, "No man is an island," and I agree wholeheartedly. We exist within relationships and everyone has a desire to have better relationships such as better spousal relationships, better parent and child relationships, better friendships and better interpersonal relationships. The closer people are to us, the stronger our desire to have a better and happier relationship with them since happiness is every human being's ultimate goal.

The strange thing about it is that while everyone wants to be happy and works hard at being happy, not everyone is able to achieve happiness. Where does the problem lie? In fact, for some people, working hard at being happy will make them unhappy, the harder they work at being happy, the more unhappy they become and therefore, we always hear things like, "I loved him/her so much, why does he/she still behave this way?" "I tried so hard but he/she still treats me this way." "Where did I go wrong? What is the cause of the problem?"

Therefore, just having love and just working hard at being happy is not enough. We have to love in the correct way and we have to master the knowledge of love and understand the mysteries of relationships.

What is the secret behind helping children to develop a love for learning?
A good parent and child relationship.

What is the most important key to enjoying great wealth and happiness?
A good relationship with one's mother and respect and filial piety towards one's parents.

What is the most important foundation for a successful marriage?
Respecting each other's parents and family.

If you already knew the answers to the above questions, I congratulate you! You have already started to experience the wonders of relationships. This book will help to deepen your experience so that you can confidently help yourself and others create a better future. If you were not able to answer the above questions, then this book will open another door in your life and lead you towards success and happiness.

Other than the superficial interactions we have with each other, our relationships are also affected by the deeper workings of our mind. However, we often only see what is on the surface and get stuck in the superficial aspect of the problem. Just like how we would only see the tip of an iceberg, we are unable to see the deeper truths about the relationship. As a result, we tend to love in the wrong way or move in the wrong direction, causing both parties to be unhappy as we create more disharmony and distance within the relationship, sometimes even to the extent of creating family pain and tragedy. Is there any way to help us understand the deeper workings of the relationship between family members? Is there a way we could understand how our children are feeling? Is it possible to understand the communication that is taking place between couples on a deeper level? Are we able to understand the truth behind the unexplainable emotions and behaviors that we see and feel?

The answer is yes. The research related to the psychology of humans and their deeper relationships is what Systemic Constellations is all about.

Understanding Systemic Constellations

What Is A 'System'?

The general system theory proposed by the biologist von Bertalanffy in 1934 (von Bertalanffy, 1972). Everyone is living within a system. First and foremost, we have to understand what constitutes a system.

From the smallest systems like our body system and our family system, to the bigger systems like the ecological system, the national system and even the universal solar system, everything is made up of systems.

Simply put, a system is the amalgamation of a few individual objects. But the sum of all these objects is much more than all these individual items put together. Just what is this extra bit about? The "extra" is their "relationship with each other".

These objects interconnect and have now become an organic whole by itself. They interact with each other in their own way and start to affect each other. Because of this, when one object changes, the others will change too. A system that is alive is much like a live human being.

Take our body system for example. It is much more than our body parts, organs and tissues put together. It can breathe, it can move. Every cell interacts with and affects each other. If a person has a weak heart, it will affect the blood circulation throughout the whole body. If you injure one leg, not only will that affect your other limbs when you walk, it may also affect your posture, thus affecting your whole-body system.

Another example would be the family system which is made up of parents and their children. When the parents are having a quarrel, should the mother be unhappy and feel anger towards the father but suppresses her emotion to withhold herself from expressing her emotions, the child might also feel anger towards the father for no good reason (von Bertalanffy, 1972).

Even if the child did not witness the quarrel, because the child has taken on the anger of his mother, he starts to disrespect his father and starts to lose interest in school. This is the result of systems!

Parents and their children form a system. This system is affected by the hidden dynamics within the family. Should these parents try to seek help, they are likely to focus on the fact that their son has lost interest in school and plays truant. Despite investing money, time and effort on trying to resolve the issue of their son playing truant and becoming aggressive and angry, they are likely to see very little results. Because they are unaware of the hidden dynamics in the system, they will be unable to resolve the root of it-- the hidden conflict between them.

Therefore, regardless of the type of system, as long as the system is alive, every member within the system will contribute to development of the system and every member will play a part in the important events taking place within the system.

But how do the individual members of the system operate with each other?

The members actually operate with each other through their sub conscious minds (A, 2017).

Since psychologist, Sigmund Freud's, discovery that the sub conscious mind plays a huge part in the actions that we take, it has since become a widely accepted concept. But wherein lies our subconscious mind?

Famous Austrian psychologist and philosopher, Martin Buber who has made great contributions in the area of social sciences, especially in the area of social psychology and social philosophy, explains the truth about the sub conscious mind in a single sentence: "The sub conscious mind does not exist within the hearts of each individual but exists **between** individuals." (Roy, 2016).

Yes, the sub conscious does not belong to any individual. It would be more accurate to say that it exists within the relationships that they have with each other and the way it operates is through **The Field** (a message field between the different members in a system) (Lewin, 1947).

For example, if you think of everyone like a personal computer, you will find that other than our basic functions and our limited memory, we can also share information through the invisible internet. We may also share collective information over the internet. Therefore, the internet is a form of information field.

The sub conscious mind is an information field. An information field that is built by a group of people would be what famous psychologist Carl Jung calls the "Collective Consciousness" (Germine, 1997).

In other words, the relationship between members of a family system is an information field and this field forms the collective consciousness of the family (Mahr, 1998).

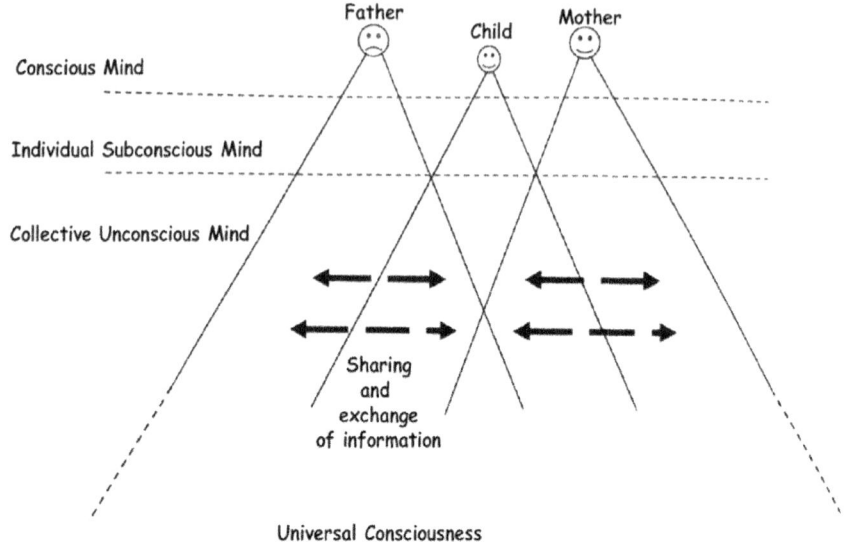

Diagram 1: Information Exchange In The Collective Unconscious Mind

But how do we observe a system's unseen information field or collective consciousness?

In actual fact, it is all around us. It is not just observable within our group minds in our cultures, our religions, popular concerts, or even election rallies, it is also in the unseen force that moves and shapes families, groups and enterprises. Suppose we go to different homes or different offices, even if we only stay for only a short while, it would be possible for us to have a feel of the general atmosphere within the family or the company. However, strange as it might be, the people who are within the system seem mostly oblivious to it. They might get a vague feel of it but will only feel and see the full effects it has on the members of the system when something serious happens to the system.

Let's go back to the previous example. The child feels anger towards his father and is unwilling to go to school. Should the child not have exhibited these behaviors, we will be unable to discover the hidden relationship problem between his parents. Therefore, the collective unconscious mind of a system is a powerful hidden force that controls everything that happens in the system. It can bring about success and can also bring about destruction. It has its own unique modus operandi and rules. What we need to investigate therefore, is the "system" and the power behind its modus operandi.
So how do we know what constitutes a system's modus operandi? Should we continue to be affected unconsciously by it? Or could we understand how it works and learn how to make things better?

Just like the internet, as long as we have the correct tools, we will be able to connect to the information field. "Systemic Constellations", is the best tool to research the dynamics hidden behind each system, the rules it operates upon and status of its collective unconscious so that we can understand its inner workings and find a way to improve upon the current situation.

The Evolution and Development of Systemic Constellations
"Systemic Constellations" began as a psychology model developed by German psychologist, Bert Hellinger (Cohen, 2006). Through the appointment of characters to set up a constellation representing various family members and interaction between the characters, it explores the current challenges in a person's life or relationship and moves the situation forward in search of a solution. The discovery of the phenomenon behind Systemic Constellations happened like this: Before the discovery of systemic constellations, a family therapy method had already existed. It requires the therapist to make an appointment with the whole family to take part in the therapy together. The family would sit down together and communicate with one another. However, someone always had some sort of last-minute engagement and would be unable to make it. And so, the therapist had to ask his assistant to take the place of this absent person, for example, the father or mother in the family. An amazing thing happened! The

therapist's assistant was able to share the emotions of the person he represented and what made it even more amazing was that the assistant had not prior knowledge about that person or his life at all.

The therapist was very curious about this phenomenon and started to conduct some experiments. His experiments proved that such a phenomenon does indeed exist. Thereafter, a female therapist in America used this as a basis to develop a prototype of the very first systemic healing model. German psychologist, Bert Hellinger, learnt the system from her and integrated it with other things he has learnt to develop Systemic Constellations. Using many families as research and experimentation, he eventually developed a workable psycho-therapy model.

Thereafter, Bert Hellinger started to demonstrate this systemic psychotherapy model in various parts of Europe. In the 1990's, Systemic Constellations sparked a wave of debate through the specialists working in helping professions all over the world. With the participation of his colleagues, this psychology model eventually became an independent school of thought in the area of applied psychology. Currently, professionals and academics from more than 30 countries in the world are learning and applying this method of healing and helping countless families and individuals with their lives (Cohen, 2006).

As with the development of all academic knowledge which is usually founded on the work that had been previously discovered, the model of Systemic Constellations also bears inputs and influences from many professional techniques and concepts used in psychological counseling. These include: Behavioral Therapy, Gestalt Therapy, Systemic Therapy, TA Communication Analysis, Hypnosis, etc. It also includes the work of many previous discoveries made by psychologists such as Ivan Boszormenyinagy's Contextual Therapy, JL Moreno's Psychological Drama and Virgina Satir's Family Therapy. What makes the model even more valuable is that Bert Hellinger also made further inputs into the model through his keen observations, his philosophical knowledge and his courageous spirit of creating something new. He summarized the basic essentials that represent "The Order of Love" and principles affecting family relationships and he continued to develop and expand the new model and the way it is being used and applied (Hellinger et al., 1998).

The Application Of Systemic Constellations
Now that you have a brief understanding about the history and development of Systemic Constellations, we will talk about the actual process of Systemic Constellations: When a client comes forward to ask for help, the constellator or facilitator will ask him to describe his or her issue. The constellator then decides what are the crucial elements related to this issue (for example, the client's father, mother or other family members) and invites some of his assistants to act as a "representative". Next, the client is asked to use his intuition and place these representatives in a position he wishes to place them, forming what would be the relationships between the characters.

The moment the representatives are put in their positions, they immediately form a relationship and an "information field" is created. The bodies then become a receptor for the deeper information within the system and will start to express what they feel. The issue that has been bugging the client will manifest itself figuratively through the positioning of the characters and the movement that takes place between them. These representatives are not informed in advance of the exercise, they are not given any information and do not have a chance to run any rehearsals. However, once they are settled down and centered, they will be able to express what they feel and think as the character they represent through their bodies in a neutral way. In this way, the dynamics of the relationship become very clear. The constellator would explore and guide them in the process and very often, a solution will present itself (Hellinger et al., 1998).

This may sound very magical but if you have personally been involved in the process, you will realize that this is true. These biological messages exist universally for us to observe. To be very precise, **Systemic Constellations is the usage of the scientific phenomena of an information field**. Using the human body as an information receptor and an information transmitter, we explore the information and the influences it has on the changes that take place within the system. The use of this scientific phenomenon to explore relationships has been taking place for more than 30 years and it has seen countless cases of successful counseling. At present, there are also many scientists researching on this science about biological information and its various aspects. (Sheldrake, 1995) [1]

Walsh (2005) concluded that because information exists between the individual elements in a system, therefore, the research about Systemic Constellations is not only linked to the psychology of the individual elements, but is also linked to the psychology of the whole system. It allows what famous psychologist, Carl Jung, terms as "collective unconscious" to present itself in a way that can be seen and felt, allowing us to understand how this collective unconscious in the humankind came about and how we are affected by it. In addition, Systemic Constellations is one of the few psychology models that investigates the human psychology from the point of a whole system view to search for solutions in a holistic way. At the same time, it signifies a new era for family therapy. Through Systemic Constellations, we have discovered that many family emotions and unfinished businesses would actually transfer onto our future generations, affecting their families and the physiology and emotions of the individuals. In this context, Systemic Constellations is a very good inspection tool for family's psychological dynamics, thereby helping one to understand the family psychological state and finding a solution to improve it. Therefore, Systemic Constellations can be said

---

[1] English scientist, Ruper Sheldrake, is currently a forerunner in the area of research about the information fields. He once described the Morphic Field in this way: "Nature is not a machine and that each kind of system - from crystals to birds to societies - is shaped not by universal laws that embrace and direct all systems but by a unique "morphic field" containing a collective or pooled memory. So organisms not only share genetic material with others of their species, but are also shaped by a "field" specific to that species..."

to be a revolutionary milestone in the area of modern psychology and counseling (Essl, 2008).

Just like how metrological cloud images can show us how typhoons are formed and the speed and direction at which they are moving, Systemic Constellations acts like a satellite that is used for observing relationship systems. It can help us uncover all the deeper layers of our family, enterprise and interpersonal relationships, thus allowing us to understand which direction the system is moving towards, how the individual members of the system are interacting with each other and what are the powers that influence them. It allows us to understand how these powers can affect disputes and find a way to sort them out. Through this simple method, we can find out what are the things we have neglected and which direction we should focus our efforts on, so that all the stuck energy in our lives get a chance to start moving again.

Therefore, Systemic Constellations can be used in the areas of (Cohen, 2006) :

1. **Relationship Issues**: Supporting us to create a happier family life and creating successful spousal relationships, parent and child relationships, working relationships and also interpersonal relationships.

2. **Physical or Psychological Issues**: Supporting us to improve the management of our emotions, thereby allowing our body to grow healthily and happily. It also supports the development of our spirituality and allows better planning of our lives.

3. **Enterprise and Organizational Issues**: Supporting the development and management of enterprises by exploring the deeper dynamics within the organizations, searching for solutions, providing vital info needed before making important decisions (including understanding what might be the likely effects following the decision) and assistance for human resource management.

However, making use of the "constellation process" in Systemic Constellations to face up to our problems and search for a solution is considered a "general function". What is even more important is that we learn from the essence of Systemic Constellations, apply it to our daily lives and appreciate the truth about life and the universe, thereby creating a better and a more harmonious world. I found this is the 'greater purpose' of Systemic Constellations.

Over the years, I have expanded the usage of Systemic Constellations. Instead of merely using it in problem solving consultations, I have started to apply it also in the area of life development and personal growth. Learning from the many cases and individuals that I have worked with and using the traditional wisdom from the East, I have developed a deeper understanding of the very essence of Systemic Constellations- **The Principles of Relationships**. If we can apply these principles to our lives, it will allow us to start a metamorphosis from inside out and we will be able to help ourselves and others move towards success and happiness to create a better world, thereby fulfilling the greater purpose of Systemic Constellations.

Therefore, the true essence of Systemic Constellations is to support life and growth and to give us knowledge that allows us to move towards happiness and harmony.

The 5 Principles Of Relationships

There are hidden principles governing the function of the universe. Bert Hellinger, the founder of Family Constellations also discovered that there are hidden rules that govern human relationships (Hellinger, 2001a). Using Hellinger's discovery as a foundation, I have put together "The 5 Principles of Relationships" based on what I have learnt from the tens of thousands of cases I have facilitated and the knowledge I have about traditional eastern wisdom and modern western psychology.

These principles happen to coincide with the universal life principles that Chinese sages have come up with based on their observations about life:

Just like the Chinese Taoist Master, Lao Zi said, "Man models himself after earth, earth models itself after heaven, heaven models itself after Tao, and Tao models itself after nature." (人法地，地法天，天法道，道法自然。) The operating power behind these principles are merely an expression and integration of the principles of the "big Tao" (flow of life) and love being applied to our daily lives.

And like what Confucius has always emphasized: "Love to exist between parent and child, righteousness to exist between king and his ministers, differences to exist between man and wife, sequencing order to exist between elderly and child, trust to exist between friends." (父子有親，君臣有義，夫媳有別，長幼有序，朋友有信。), through these laws, the concrete practice of these Confucian principles has practical application in the areas of psychology, family life, interpersonal relationships and societal relationships.

Like these realizations made by the Buddha: "There exists shared karma from cause and effect" (因果共業), "The origin of the world lies in the relationships between all and the essence of the 'self' is created out of emptiness" (緣起性空) and "Acknowledging what is" (一切如是), the spirit behind these Buddhist insights are merely philosophical truths being presented in our modern languages so that these Buddhist principals can be easily understood and applied by everybody.

Therefore, these principles are natural and are not a created or invented by any individual. They are not conceived by Bert Hellinger, nor were they made up by me. They are the principles of nature and are not man made. Simply put, Principles of Relationships are just a manifestation of the principles of nature (Nelles, 2006).

So what constitutes the Principles of Relationships? I have categorized them as below:

Principle of Wholeness

We are a whole system in entirety, every member has to have a place and position in the system. This system will continue to develop and grow.

The concept of entirety is a uniquely Eastern concept and is now concurrently being rediscovered by many cultures and sciences. The concept states that wholeness exists inside all the small individual elements which make up the whole system. Through these small individual elements, you will be able to catch a glimpse of the entire system. A good example is how Auricular Acupuncture and Master Tung's Acupuncture methods in traditional Chinese medication can heal any disease in the body through diagnosis and therapy via only one's ears or hands. Thus, the concept of entirety is actually in disguise, hidden amongst all the small individual elements in the system. However, any changes in the individual element would result in changes happening in the entire system.

Similarly, relationships are actually an organic, whole system. Therefore, all that goes on within the system would be reflected within the individual members of the system. Members of the system will take on all the unfinished businesses going on in the system and therefore, the events that take place in the entire system takes precedence over its individual members. Yet at the same time, any changes within its individual members will affect the entire system (Hellinger, 2001a).

Understanding whole system of human relationships will thus deeply change the way we view things and people, especially towards unexplained emotions and behaviors and some repetitive family stories/destinies. We no longer merely look at an individual's emotions or behavior but instead, become aware of the root cause hiding behind the problem. We are thus able to make observations about these deeper influences that impact the overall system.

Furthermore, in family relationships among humans, The Principle Of Wholeness requires that anyone belonging to this family system will always have the right to belong and will always have a "place" within the family. This principle deeply influences our lives, yet it is often neglected by us. Very often, when a family member experiences a misfortune such as stillbirth, suicide or an accident, etc, we tend to unconsciously forget or exclude them from the family, just as if they never existed at all. Or perhaps when a family member's behavior does not meet the standards set within the family (they may be gamblers, alcoholics or criminals, etc), their position in the family will be excluded by other family members in their hearts.

If the above-mentioned situation arises, regardless of whether it was done intentionally or unintentionally, it is still going against the Principle of Wholeness as the principle dictates that the entire system includes every single member within and does not allow any of them to be excluded. On top of that, this information will be stored within the collective consciousness of the family and will cause the other members of the family to try to "take up the places" of those who are being excluded. When this happens, this person will unconsciously repeat the life patterns and stories of the person he or she was trying to replace. The price they have to pay would be unexplainable emotions, behaviors or sickness and in extreme cases, even death (Hellinger, 2003a).

Worth noting, however, is that all the "family system members" mentioned here are govern by certain relationship norms. Not every distant relative we have belongs to our family system. Later, we will explore and find out who are the people belonging to our family system and it will increase our understanding and awareness about whether anyone in our family is being excluded.

Principle of Order

There is a sequencing order between the elderly and the young; everyone has the right to belong.

In the relationships we have, the closest ones are those we have with the people within our family systems. The position and order of every member in the family system is as important as the gravitational force between planets within the solar system and it affects the whole system. Very often, because we are unaware of this, we are affected and pulled in by this force unconsciously.

To a family system, the Principle of Order is one of the most important principles: everyone in this family should follow an order based on their seniority and be respected according to this "arrangement". Everyone should go back to the "position" that belongs to them. Regardless of whether we are intentionally doing it, should a family go against this Principle, the disorder within the family will bring about repetitive lessons about pain and failure until we become aware of this disorder and move back into the rightful place of the order (Hellinger et al., 1998).

The concept that "there is sequencing order between the elderly and the young" (長幼有序) and that "everything has its own place to belong to" (萬物有歸) has been expounded by the great Chinese educator, Confucius, over some 2000 years ago and he believes that this is the fundamental basis of the Great Harmony Of The World. Therefore, the Principle of Order and Confucianism actually echo each other and is a modern application of the school of ethics. The characteristics of the Principle of Order can be "seen and experienced" through the use of Systemic Constellations. The process allows everyone to observe the after effects of disorder within the family and offers a physical presentation of the benefits of following the Principle of Order. Because regardless of whether people assign a great value to it or choose to blatantly ignore it, the Principle of Order does not stop working. Eventually disorder always brings about serious consequences again and again.

Through the many real life examples being presented in this book, we will start to understand the power behind the Principle of Order and how these members of the system affect each other. It is then possible for us to become aware if we are in the right position in the order and whether the interactions taking place between family members are harmonious and following the correct order.

Therefore, learning and applying the Principle of Order allows us to determine our position in the system. We can then remind ourselves to love from our own position and transform our small, blind love into a mature, big love, transforming failure into success so that we can once again have a taste of happiness. If we can understand the essence of the Principle of Order and apply it in our interpersonal relationships, our jobs and our enterprises, it will help to create a more harmonious and orderly society.

Principle Of Balance

There has to be a balance between giving and receiving.

The Principle of Balance is one of the most important principles of nature. Since the start of time, nature has maintained a delicate balance. The interactions between humans rise out of the instinct to balance things out. The balance between giving and receiving is the secret behind a successful relationship. But the art of balance requires much practice.

When someone is good to us, we have to reciprocate by giving them back a little bit more than what they have given us. Likewise, we will also need to learn how to respond to negative treatment, by returning slightly less than what they gave us while "sending love along" with it. Therefore the Principle of Balance is not about glossing over things and pretending to be in peace but rather, to act as a foundation that allows relationships to interact with each other in a more genuine way.

So how do you balance out between parent and child? Hellinger (2001b) said that there will never be a balance between parent and child because our parents have given us the most precious gift- our lives. We can never do the same and give birth to our parents and thereby, it is naturally imbalanced. However, we can choose to be like our parents and pass this life on to our children while we continue to be filial to our parents. This becomes a balance within the fluidity of life.

In addition, there needs to be a balance when it comes to money and responsibility. All moneys gained from dishonest means, hurt and fraud will eventually create some form of impact on our family systems. We will eventually have to pay the price through negative impact on our bodies, minds or career. This observation coincides with the principle of Cause And Effect expounded by Buddhism. Just like the Buddhist Masters have said, "All phenomena end with emptiness; only cause and effect end with its influence." (萬法皆空, 因果不空). Therefore, the requirement of balance within relationships is not merely a human instinct but also a foundation for the interactions of life.

This principle is not limited to the interactions that take place in our family and with the people we meet but is also applicable at work, in office, in a country, in our society and even in nature. It is a principle that even the relationship between heaven, humans, things and one's self has to adhere strictly to (Hellinger, 2003b; Hellinger, 2003c; Payne, 2005).

Principle Of Reality

There is a need to respect and acknowledge the reality as it is.

To "respect and acknowledge the reality of things as it is" means that we link up with life. It means we are can face up to, integrate and accept everything that is happening in the world right now and accept the truth as it is. Reality is often the best teacher; it is the strongest power that accelerates our growth. Therefore, facing up to the reality as it is will allow us to take the most suitable or best possible action at home, in life and at work. Everyone in the system needs to face up to reality and respect and acknowledge reality as it is.

This is easier said than done. And it is especially so for issues related to unexpected family tragedies. For example, if a little boy were to meet with a traffic accident and die, his father might have a strong fear that the same thing might happen to his other children. As a result, he may hide all the photos of the son who passed away so as not to let the other children know that they had this elder brother. But the price of hiding the truth is that the children who are born after that will have a huge danger of getting into a traffic accident as well. The father will also continue to feel lots of fear about this and when he does a Systemic Constellations, he will be able to see that the outcome of denying this truth is that his other children will unconsciously want to follow their elder brother and move towards the path of death.

The father then realizes the impact of his decision to hide the truth. Once he is back home, he immediately tells his other children about this brother of theirs and decides to make it a family project to do something good together in memory of this dead brother.

Once the truth is being acknowledged, the chance of the other children meeting with a traffic accident immediately becomes much smaller. This is because when a family is unwilling to acknowledge reality and tries to use some weird ways to run away from it, neglect it or negate it, this incident becomes an unfinished business in the family system. Like a black hole in the system, it will constantly affect this family. On the contrary, if we just accept reality, we will be able to bring in release and healing energy into the system, thereby opening a door for of possibility for the resolution of this unfinished business (Nelles, 2006).

Respecting and acknowledging reality includes "respecting the true identity of every single person in the family system". And 'verbalizing aloud" is an important way to show acknowledgement. For example, the child might say to his father, "You are my father and I am your son. You are my elder and I am your junior." Or in another case, the second wife says to the ex-wife of her husband, "You are his first wife, I am his second wife. You came before me." When these words are spoken aloud from the heart, it means that the person who says it understands reality and acknowledges it. This will bring a sense of stability and release to everyone involved in this system.

This may look easy but in actual fact, we often refuse to acknowledge our family and their identities because of their behaviours. The most common example takes place when a couple is in a fight or has separated. It is very easy for one party to unconsciously reject the other person.

For example, they may say to their child, "Your father is irresponsible, he is not fit to be your father." Or "Your mother is a bad woman; she doesn't want you and ran away with someone else." When we reject a person and their identity, everybody in the system, especially the children, will feel a sense of unease and they may thus exhibit inappropriate behaviour or emotions and repeat the patterns of unhappiness taking place within the family. (We will discuss this further in Chapter 4: Parent and Child Relationships.) Therefore, following the rules that control our lives, we need to learn that the truth does not change just because we refuse to accept or acknowledge it.

In addition to that, in refusing to accept or acknowledge reality, not only do we end up having to pay a high price, we also lose a chance to learn the lesson that life has given us.

Principle Of Flow

Information about relationships will be passed on from generations to generations, the vitality of life should be always flowing forward.

Life is constantly moving in a flow. It makes use of every individual living thing as an information receptor and transmitter and uses their constant interaction to pass on messages within the group. The same can be said for what happens in our family, company or society. Because life is passed down from generations to generations, the information within the systems will also be passed down through the generations. The information being passed on is way beyond what we can conceive. It includes emotions, beliefs, behavioural patterns, physical conditions, knowledge and intuition, destiny and fate, etc and the "collective consciousness" - a database of information shared between humankind and a powerful experience library accumulated by our forefathers- that psychologist, Carl Jung was talking about. It can be said that all the information about life is being passed on through relationships (Germine, 1997).

Therefore, we need to understand that as information will always be passed down to the next generation, everything that happened to our ancestors would affect us as well. Anything that is "unfinished" in your generation will also be passed down to the future generations.

This will help us develop awareness and this awareness will help us in respecting the fates of our family histories while deriving much learning and strength from it. We start to become accountable for ourselves, stop life from flowing backwards and move it forward in a flow. We become aware of the entanglements and disputes in the family and we can thus transform this into a supporting strength for the family to move towards success and happiness. This is the power of the Principle of Flow.

So, what happens if we go against the Principle of Flow?

This means that our life force is not flowing forward but flowing backwards. For example, we may give up having our own family because we need to take care of our original family or perhaps we are unable to pass life on to the next generation. If we constantly hanker after the past and are unable to see the relationships in front of us, we will be unable to inject our life force to the present.

For example, the family may have some huge trauma and part of our energy may become frozen in that particular time and space or we may suffer from post-traumatic stress and be unable live on with complete life force. All these go against the Principle of Flow and the outcome is that the future generations will have to take on the emotions, imbalances and entanglements (Levine, 2005).

The same pattern will keep repeating generation after generation and our life force would be unable to perform to its maximum potential. And when the life force in the family starts to shrink, there starts to be a decline in the number of future generations and everything will eventually come to an end (Ulsamer, 2005).

The Principle of Flow emphasizes that life has to flow forward always. We should let bygones be bygones and live totally in the present. We should also pass life on to our future generations because in actual fact, the information being passed on within families is also a form of love. Through our heritage of life, we can pass our love on to the future generations. The blood of our ancestor's flow within us and has been passed on for generations.

The many experiences and knowledge of our ancestors will make the very best treasure box of wisdom. If we are humble, we will be able to draw out the essence of this wisdom and through the flexible usage of this essence and hard work, we can create unlimited potential for ourselves and our future generations.

The 5 principles mentioned are also the principles of life. Feeding on the essence of the wisdom of our forefathers, it has gone beyond time and space and is applicable in all situations. Regardless of how much time has gone by and how many regimes have been changed, they will continue to be preserved because they are the truth. They are the manifestation of the principles of nature and the most primordial desire of life.

The value of these principles lies in their practicality. If we can thoroughly understand these principles and apply them while confidently walking towards love, our love will be nurtured and expanded in our relationships and we will start to awaken within love.

Reviewing Your Relationship

Now, we understand the 5 Principles of Relationship and understand how Systemic Constellations can help us gain more awareness of what is going on in the inner depths of our minds and our families. When we come across blind spots and get into a situation where "The person on the spot is baffled but the onlooker sees it clearly" (a Chinese saying: 當局者迷，旁觀者清), Systemic Constellations can help us see the truth of the matter and find ways to improve the situation. More importantly, it can help us understand the lessons we can learn from these challenges.

Here are some questions you can ask yourself:

Do you know what are the lessons you have to learn from your relationships?

Do you know what are the lessons you have to learn from this life?

Some people may find out their life lessons and life mission very quickly. Confucius discovered his life's destiny at the age of 50, what about us?

I have seen many people living till the end of their lives repeating the same patterns and challenges. Yet, they were unable to learn from them and change the outcome. However, as long as we are willing to learn and pick up excellent knowledge like the psychology of Systemic Constellations, it will support us in our exploration into our deeper psychological state and we will be able to understand the deeper meanings behind our relationships and appreciate the important lessons in our lives. In short, we will be able to find a better way to love and to live life.

Now, let us take a moment to review your relationship. There will be 5 questions and I would like you to answer them one by one. Pause for a few seconds at each question and remember to listen to your heart. After which, write down the answer that you hear from your heart:

Do you feel any hatred or guilt towards anybody? Do you have any unfinished business with anybody?

-- When I ask this question, who is it that comes to your mind?

Are you in the right position and order in your family?

-- Do you know all the members in your family?

Are you aware if you are feeling peace within your heart?

-- What did you observe within your heart?

Did you desire to love someone but put it on hold? -- When I asked you this question, what came into your mind?

Have you fulfilled all your wishes and are without any regrets? -- What is your answer?

If you can really quieten down and face up to these questions honestly, you might be surprised to discover what your inner self is trying to communicate with you. All these are possible causes of unfinished business. If you respect yourself, you would treasure these messages and try to find solutions and a method to complete the affinity you have with these people.

Many people have heard of this story: A man had the great honour of visiting hell and heaven. He saw tonnes of delicious food being laid on the tables of hell but the people sitting round the tables were all skin and bones and they looked really depressed. Everyone can see the food in front of them but are unable to eat them. That's because they are all holding very long spoons in their hands. While they can scoop up the food, they are unable to put them into their own mouths. Next, he visits heaven. There are also lots of delicious foods on the table and the people were also using the same long spoons. But he discovered one stark difference and that is, in heaven, "everyone feeds someone else" so everyone gets to enjoy a sumptuous meal.

In actual fact, depending on how we choose, our world can become heaven or hell. If we can learn to support each other and nurture each other in our relationships, the real-life examples in this book will be a great revelation that will help us find a way to complete our relationships. Then, we will be able to create a heaven on earth.

Chapter 2: Relationships Between Men And Women

The way of great human is started from the relationship between husband and wife. When you fulfill its utmost, you will understand the wisdom of universe.
    --Confucius

君子之道，造端乎夫婦，及其至也，察乎天地。
    --孔子

Men and Women: Different, Yet Complimentary Parts Of A Whole

The I Ching states, "The birth of all things come from the interaction between heaven and earth, yin and yang." (天地以陰陽交媾而生萬物) Men and women are attracted to each other because of nature's blessing-- sexual energy. Just like flowers blooming beautifully and a peacock brilliantly opening up its feathers, The Great Nature's sexual energy has created many good things in this world. Sexual energy allows a person to take form and all of us have life because of it. Sexual energy is therefore the vital and most important basis for the formation of life.

Hellinger (2001b) pointed out that when men and women attract each other, on a deeper level, they are in fact attracted by each other's sexual energy. Just like the positive and negative pole in magnets and the north and south poles in the earth's magnetic field, when a man is attracted to a woman, it is because he feels that the woman has something that he lacks. Similarly, the woman feels incomplete and is attracted to the man because he seems to have that special something that will complete her. When both of them have the missing piece and is willing to provide what the other party needs, both parties will complement the other party and complete each other to become one whole.

But we all know that even with nature's sexual energy helping us, the relationship between man and woman is not without obstacles and does not bear fruit overnight. Rather, one needs to carefully manage it over time. Facing up to and overcoming challenges is a basic part of life and the relationship between couples is not exempted from this. We need to develop our ability to constantly make adjustments and solve problems. The relationship between man and woman is a reality of life. Having a successful relationship with one's partner is considered one of the epitomes of success.

However, as the saying goes, "Men are from Mars and women are from Venus". With all the glaring differences between men and women, just how do we get along, how do we love each other? Is there any rule we could follow to make our love more successful?

During Systemic Constellations, we always notice that there seems to be a set of principles that all relationships operate by and that is the "Principles of Relationships". It does not just affect the people who are related to us by blood but also the non-blood-related people who have an intimate relationship with us. Regardless of whether we are conscious about it, problems and issues in a relationship very often stem from the fact that the relationship is going against Principles of Relationships. Principles of Relationships do not follow a hard and fast rule and every couple is considered a unique and different case. But one thing we can be sure of is that all couples must understand and follow Principles of Relationships. Only then, will they be able to avoid lots of conflict and pain and only then can they help themselves walk out of pain to enjoy the happiness and joys of a more intimate relationship.

The relationship principles that bind a couple in an intimate relationship are as follows (Hellinger, 2001b) :

1. The basic requirements men and women should have of each other is this: Men should want her "because she is a woman" and women should want him because "he is a man". Should they be together for some other reason such as wanting to save the other party or feeling pity, their connection will not be able to develop further.

2. Joining through love and sex (or sometimes just purely through sex) can allow two partners to bond. Every bonding that takes place in the sequence of your life has to be acknowledged, every one of your partners and their "sequential order and position" has to be respected.

3. Respect the differences between the two genders. Respect that these differences have the same value and accept your unique characteristics as a man or a woman. Only then can your love grow and develop out of this respect.

4. There has to be a balance in the interaction between giving and receiving.

5. Both partners need to accept and respect the truth of not just their own family but also that of their partner's family.

The above-mentioned rules and phenomena affect all intimate relationships deeply. They are the source of most issues that a couple might face. Most of the time, we only see the devastating results of not following these rules but if we can start to understand and become aware of them, we will be able to review our relationship with our partners and see the relationship and its challenges in different light.

Respecting Sequence, Balancing The Two Sexes

There was once a man who told Bert Hellinger that he would like to find a woman who can develop a stable relationship with him. Hellinger asked him how many previous partners he had and he answered that he had 7 previous partners. Hellinger told him then, to forget the idea of finding a woman who can develop a stable relationship with him. The man refused to give up and asked if there was any way he could rectify the situation. Hellinger replied, "The only chance you ever have of fulfilling your wish is this: If you can respect all your 7 former partners, receive all the love they had given you and keep all this love inside your heart and bring this love as a gift into your new relationship, then you will have a chance to develop a stable and lasting relationship." (Hellinger, 2001a).

Through the "Principle of Wholeness" and "Principle of Order", we notice that only when the relationships with the exes have all been accepted and respected, then will the relationships with future partners be able to develop successfully.

In this way, the value of the former partners can be recognized and both parties would be able to go on their separate ways peacefully without any entanglements or unfinished business.

Furthermore, from the "Principles of Balance", we can see that when there is imbalance in the relationship, there will be an underlying force that will try to correct the imbalance. Therefore, when couples who are responsible for the imbalance do not take up the responsibility to restore balance, the ones that will pay the sorry price will be their future generations.

A good example is this: during one of my workshops, there was a couple who had a very good relationship with each other. They loved their son very much but for some unknown reason, their son often seems to hold a hidden aggression towards his mother and even tried to threaten her. Nothing had happened between them previously but this aggression seems to dictate the attitude the son had towards his mother. They have communicated and discussed extensively about this issue but to no avail.

Through a Systemic Constellations process, we discovered that the mother had an ex-boyfriend who parted with her on bad terms. When they broke up, she was very unfair to him and had caused him much pain. As a result, the ex-boyfriend felt lots of resentment towards her.

During the constellations, we discovered that the son of this particular couple actually shared the same expression of anger as the particular ex-boyfriend! It was as if he has taken over the ex-boyfriend's emotions and therefore, he had an attitude of resentment towards his mother.

When the mother saw how the representative who represented her son was having the same expression of anger as her ex-boyfriend, she was in total shock. But of course, in our daily lives, no one will be able to observe this similarity; we will only be able to see the effects of it.

Now that we have discovered the root of the problem, what do we do next? Firstly, I had the mother apologize to her ex-boyfriend while she affirms and respect the love he had for her. I got her to treasure the time they spent together and requested that she gives this love a space in her heart and hide it there. I also got her to apologize for the hurt she has caused and got them to both take up their individual responsibility for what had happened. Eventually, there was a peaceful resolution.

Next, we allowed the son to go back to his rightful place in the family and we got the mother to tell him clearly, "You are my son, I am your mother, whatever happened between me and my ex-boyfriend has got nothing to do with you. You are the son of me and your father." Right after that, the anger the son had for his mother disappeared quickly and the interactions between mother and son started to improve immediately.

From this example and the next real-life example I am going to share, we have proven that the Principles of Relationships between men and women is such that it has to always be in balance. Even if both parties were to break up, they have to do so in a way that balance is restored. If not, this entanglement will be brought forward to the future generations and these innocent kids would get all entangled in it. Also, every position in the sequential order has to be respected and acknowledged, that includes ex partners and their children. It is important to accept both sides of the family as they are.

All these will lay the best foundation and allow the love between a man and woman to grow.

Extramarital Affair, It Happened To Me

Deep and intense relationships with our partners do not come about by chance. It is the reward for achieving a certain state of maturity in our spiritual growth. At the same time, it is like a door that allows us to connect with the essence of life through our partners (Hellinger, 2001a).

The following is a case of participating in my systemic constellation workshop. The same applies to all the cases provided later.

Chen Xin is a very refined woman. With her copper toned skin and well-maintained figure, she gives one an impression of being a very strong and masculine woman in her simple and neat outfit. However, her hair is in a mess and there was a look of helplessness about her. She is a participant in my workshop but has been moodily keeping to herself all the while.

On the third day of the workshop, she happened to sit next to me. I looked at her downturned mouth and asked her, "What happened?"

With a tad of embarrassment, she shared about her problem with me. "My husband and I have a problem with our sex life."

"What do you mean by that?"

Chen Xin turned a deeper shade of red and revealed, "I would like to have make love with my husband but he does not have any reaction."

"How do you express your desire for sex?"

"I just sleep closer to him."
I smiled and asked her, "Does your husband know that you want to have make love with him?"
Chen Xin nodded her head, "I should think so."
"Okay, let's explore where the problem lies and how to rectify it. Please choose one of the participants to represent your husband. Then give him a position within this classroom. You will then move to your

own position so that your positions depict the relationship between the two of you.

Chen Xin placed her husband in front of her, face to face. Their distance between them was about 1 meter apart.

At this moment, something interesting happened. Chen Xin wanted to move closer to her husband but her husband continued to keep a distance. The more eager she was to close up the distance, the bigger distance he wanted to keep between them. Chen Xin started to get impatient and worried...

I asked the person representing her husband what he felt and he said, "I feel that she does not respect me!"

The moment he uttered those words, "Does not respect me", Chen Xin's eyes turned red and started to tear.

I looked at her and asked her, "What happened?"

The strong woman before me broke down and cried but she still tried to retain her composure by trying to speak normally, "Since that incident from three years ago, my life has totally changed..." Instead of answering my question, she wiped away her tears and said, "My life has been a mess in the past three years."

So I prompted her gently, "What happened three years ago?"

She wiped away her tears, took a deep breath and finally said, "My husband had an extramarital affair." Tears started to cascade uncontrollably down her face as she continued, "Perhaps I had been too strong and controlling over him. He always complained that he is not given a chance to make any decisions at home. In our 10 years of marriage, most of the decisions at home were made by me. My husband started to travel overseas because of work and I started to notice that he was behaving strangely. Eventually, he admitted that there was a third party in our relationship... it was so difficult for me to accept the truth of it... I never thought that this would ever happen to me."

"Oh! So that is it. Your lack of sexual intimacy was just a surface phenomenon but the real issue is that there is an "imbalance" in your relationship. Because you do not respect him and give him a position in the family, he made use of abstinence from "sex" and an extramarital affair to retaliate. It is a pity though. "Revenge strategies" like these do not bring about any resolution to the issue at all. So when you found out about the affair, how did you react?"

Chen Xin paused for a few moments, shook her head and said, "I tried to hurt myself, I ruined my life and even once thought of ending it."

In any relationship, when the person who is being victimized does not fight back or revenge but instead, lets themselves lead terrible lives, this is as good as aggravating the pain and "injury" so that the other party does not get a chance to compensate for it. Deep inside them, this is what these victims are thinking: "I am better than you are and so I will not retaliate but the hurt you have placed upon me will never be erased." In actual fact, this is a form of revenge and this passive aggression will create even more problems for the relationship. Should these people choose to break up and go their separate ways, they would still never come to a resolution.

I told Chen Xin, "You have to make some adjustments and balance out your relationship. At the start, you show disrespect towards your husband and your husband makes use of sex and an extramarital affair to retaliate. Following that, you hurt yourself to get back at him. But this is the worst possible course of action to take. You will not only deepen the hurt; you are also taking away the chance that allows your husband to make up for his mistake."

"It all happened so quickly and I did not know what to do."

"No, you do know what to do. But you have to stand in your position and respond in an appropriate manner. If not, you will end up secretly manipulating your son. What do think your son will think of that in future when he finds out?"
Chen Xin quickly said, "I want my son to love his dad."

"Should you harm yourself, do you really think your son will listen to you? How do you think he will respond?" I questioned her.

Chen Xin kept silent.

I asked her, "Do you want to know what might happen?"

She nodded her head.

I continued, "This is as good as you saying to your son, "This is all your dad's fault, but please love the person who harmed me." I think if that is the case, your son will either end up becoming psychologist or contracting a neurotic disorder!"

Chen Xin paused for a moment to think and she continued slowly, "So you mean to say that I should face up to my husband and tell him how I feel?"

I nodded my head. "Let's try tat."

I asked one of the participants to represent their son and the moment the son was placed inside the constellation, he started to clench his fists and glare angrily at the father.

I pointed to the son and said to Chen Xin, "Do you see that? When you run away and are unwilling to face up to the situation, your child will take on the anger you feel towards your husband."

"Then what should I do?"

"You have to face up to this yourself and express your true emotions."

After some hesitation, Chen Xin started to tremble. Her legs were shaking terribly. It was as if she went back to the time where the incident happened. All the anger, fear and helplessness just gushed out of her heart and she almost fell flat on the floor with all the emotions. I gently supported her and reminded her to face up to the issue courageously. Finally, she could face her husband and shout out all her anger.

"I am so angry with you! Why did you have an affair... I hate you! I hate you!" She started to choke and she kept pounding her fists on her husband's body.

"I hate you, I hate you..." Chen Xin continued to hit him and wail till her voice turned hoarse.

Then, something miraculous happened. The very angry son unclenched his fist and stopped looking angry. He took a deep breathe and started to look very relieved. He then started to move to his position as a child by the side.

"Did you see the change happening to your son?" I asked her.

Chen Xin nodded.

She couldn't help but sob uncontrollably at that point. All the deep sadness within her flowed out with her tears as she pounded her fists on her husband's chest agitatedly shared her deepest feeling, "I love you, me and our son, we both love you..."" Even though her husband did not make her any promises, he looked deeply into her eyes no matter how she hit him. He never took his eyes off her while she released all those suppressed emotions, she has hidden within her heart for three whole years. After a few minutes, she gradually stopped crying.

Yes, it is very important for us to go back to our own position and it is necessary and healthy for us to express our emotions in an appropriate manner. The more important issue though, is that we can reconcile- to acknowledge the truth of what happened and take up our own responsibility for it. I guided Chen Xin to move toward reconciliation and asked her to apologize to her husband, "I am sorry I did not respect you. Sorry!"

"I am sorry I did not respect you. Sorry!" said Chen Xin. But the person representing the husband felt that she was not sincere enough.

"Yes, you cannot lie. If you really want to resolve this issue, you have to apologize sincerely."

"I am sorry I did not respect you. Sorry!" said Chen Xin repeated again. This time, we could all feel her sincerity.

Next, she made a bow to her husband. "I am sorry I did not respect your male pride. Now I can see you and I will respect your male pride."

Her husband started to turn around to face her again.

I continued to guide Chen Xin along, "You made a mistake, me too. I am willing take back the responsibility belonging to me for what went wrong in our relationship."

"Towards your affair, I am still unable to forgive you for it. I return your part of the responsibility in this issue to you."

"Yes, I made a mistake too," her husband replied and started behave in a more friendly way.

Chen Xin continued. "Thank you for all the contributions you have made to this family. I never really treasured them and now, I see all your effort."

The husband's face started to loosen up.

"Please accept me as your wife. I would like to continue to be with you."

Very slowly, her husband moved towards her. They gazed into each other's eyes. There was no deceit, no games between them. In the end, the constellations came to a peaceful end.

After that, I told Chen Xin, "Now do you know what you should do when you go back home?"

Chen Xin gave an affirmative nod, "Yes, I know what to do."

Then she asked me, "I recalled that when we got to know each other, he already had a girlfriend whom he was about to marry. I was like his extramarital affair. Is that the root of the problem?"

I replied, "It is easy to use retribution to explain this situation but what is more important is that we learn the lesson behind it. If not, these incidents will repeat themselves in our lives. Do you know what is the lesson behind this issue?"

Chen Xin gave it a thought and replied, "Respect my husband's position in the family, go back to my position in the family and find a good way to interact while keeping balance."

"Yes," I replied. "But you are also right about the ex-girlfriend. Based on my experience from the thousands of cases I have facilitated and Principles of Relationships, the both of you owe this former girlfriend of your husband an apology and some respect."

Chen Xin asked, "Then what can I do about this?"

"The most important thing is the respect you have for her in your heart. Respect that she is your husband's ex-partner and that she came before you and that you came after her. At the same time, apologize to her and beseech her to be friendly and kind towards you."

"Do I have to apologize to her in person?"

"The details can be decided based on your individual situation. The most important aspect of this is that you are sincere."

Chen Xin nodded her head. "Ok, I know what to do now."

Finally, I gave her a mysterious smile and asked her, "Do you know what the best form of revenge is?"

Chen Xin thought for a while and shook her head.

"That is to allow yourself to become even more successful, more attractive and happier!"

We smiled at each other.

A year later, Chen Xin attended an advance family constellation training I was teaching. She had become radiantly happy. She said after our workshop, she gave it a hard thought and decided not to run away from her problem. Previously, she did not want to face up to her marriage problems but ever since the workshop, things have changed. Firstly, she got in touch with her true emotions and expressed them. She cried lots but it was important that she also returned to her position as the wife. She started to become considerate towards her husband, treated him well and started to display her feminine energy fully.

"In the past, I always felt like I was his mother or the Queen of the family. I was totally not in the position of the wife. It was so tiring!" Chen Xin said.

She discovered that when she started to respect her husband's male pride, the feminine energy inside her started to become more complete. She observed that her husband started to spend more time with her and even started to smile more. He was also more willing to share how he felt with her.

In the end, she also wrote a letter of apology to her husband's ex-girlfriend. She apologized for what happened sincerely. As for the affair, she decided to return her husband's part of his responsibility to him. She has already made her stand and her husband has to take up the responsibility that belongs to him. She said when she made this decision, she felt as if a rock was lifted off her and it felt so good to let it go.

"Teacher (Chinese people tend to call their teachers or mentors that), I listened to you and committed to my own happiness and to leading a better life. I am constantly upgrading myself and learning new things so that I can be beautiful from inside out. I have also started to be more filial towards my parents. I know I used to behave rather badly

towards them but now, I am starting to really respect and care for them. I make an effort to spend time with them and buy things for them. Also, my interpersonal relationships have also improved, my friends say I seem to have become a totally different person and they even commented that I am starting to exude the charm of a mature woman. Now, my husband is the one who is afraid I might run off!" shared Chen Xin happily.

"Also, I would like to share another piece of good news. As my husband is so pleasantly surprised by my change after the workshop, I was thinking that once the time is right, I will invite him to attend a workshop since he seems to be somewhat interested in psychology too. My gut feel is that he should be ready to attend the workshop very soon."

"Good, just respect his decision," I smiled as I replied.

About Extramarital Affairs

"Extramarital affairs" are one of the most common issues between couples. Let's give it a good thought.

Does a person have the right to hold on to someone else forever?

When our partner develops another relationship with a third party, what sort of damage does it actually create?

When we develop a relationship with a third party, how does it affect us?

When a couple decides to only love each other deeply, what makes up the strength that is internally generated within them?

When an extra marital affair happens, if the innocent half does not use love to fight for the return of their other half and chooses, instead, to be both rude and overbearing, or to harass and pester the other party, do you think the other party will want to come back to them? Or perhaps, even if the person comes back physically, their heart will still be somewhere else? In extreme cases, people hurt themselves or try to kill themselves to get their partners to come back to them. Not only will the guilty half never be able to come back, all the hurt and pain will even be passed on to the future generations. As a result, the whole family will never be able to reconcile and never be able to feel peace in their hearts (Hellinger, 2001a).

Towards this, my suggestion is to opt for a more tolerant and humbler approach. Loyalty has to stem out of true love and not possession. Life has too many mysteries beyond our understanding. How do we meet our other halves? What sort of affinity draws us together and makes us husband and wife? What do we have to learn from each other? We will never be able to force our other half to make us the ONLY important person in their world. Likewise, they cannot expect that from us as well. And the matter of fact is, we will be attracted to other people and will be attracted by beautiful people and the same goes for our other half too. In fact, in the different stages of life, we will meet different people who are important in our lives and create different destinies with them. We have to respect that life is just the way it is and respect the fact that everyone is part of a sequential order while we manage our interactions to maintain balance. Only then, will we be able to find good solutions. When things happen, only love filled with wisdom can help us turn the crisis around.

The Deep Fear of Abandonment

Hellinger (2001e) from conducting the Systemic Constellations process on couples, we observed this: For many couples, when their other half is involved with a third party, they will feel a strong sense of abandonment or even a deep fear which feels like being on the brink of death because losing the other half feels as if they are about to lose their lives. This is a helpless sort of response, which is similar to that which a child feels when being abandoned by their mother. It doesn't matter what age this person is now but their sense of reliance on their partners is still child-like. Mature adults know that this issue is merely about whether their partner leaves or stays and not about life and death at all. Therefore, as long as a person requires their other half to play the role of the mother, then, regardless of whether they are male or female, their unconscious need for their partner to take on the role of the mother will bring about grave danger to their relationship. This is because, such a relationship is imbalanced. It does not allow one's partner to keep the balance in the relationship as they interact with us. Therefore, they can only choose to leave in the end. Alternatively, they may also agree to play the role of the mother but they will go outside of the relationship to find a partner who can play the role of an equal partner and can interact with them to have a relationship that is in balance.

Therefore, only when both parties are searching for an equal partner and not a mother will their relationship be able to function successfully. When you want to be in an intimate relationship with someone, you need to respect them and see them for who they are and at the same time, it is important to be aware of the dynamics that are taking place deep within yourself. This is the biggest challenge faced by all couples. As the saying goes, "Open one eye and close one eye" (a Chinese saying that means to be forgiving) but please remember my take on this-- "Open one eye to look at your partner and close one eye to look within yourself." The most important thing is to look at your other half with love. Only then, will you have a chance to see a woman or a man.

Recognition and Forgiveness of An Extramarital Affair

When a person has an affair, feels guilt and decides to openly admit it to their partner, their partner will then be forced to take responsibility for the consequences. This is a way of pushing the consequence over to the other party (the ball is now in your court) and it is a way of openly damaging the relationship because information that is so private and confidential should be protected (Mahr, 1998).

With regards this, I would like to share one of Bert Hellinger's valuable insights: "The appropriate way to deal with this situation is that the person who is feeling the guilt allows things to move back into the correct order and he or she will bear the responsibility for the consequences all by himself/herself. In this way, it will not burden other people. If they want to make up for their behavior, they can do so secretly by doing some good things for their partner. There is no need for a confession at all. This might already resolve the issue and it is a better strategy as compared to giving a full confession and creating a big *exposé*. In actual fact, when we ask for forgiveness from the other party, we are in fact pushing the responsibility of dealing with the whole situation to the other party."

So do we forgive the other party? When our partner gets into an affair, if we behave as if we graciously forgive them without fussing over it, it means we think that we are more superior than our other half and in forgiving them, we are actually making them small. This is actually a form of attack on the ego of the other party that requires the forgiveness. Therefore, this sort of forgiveness will end up bringing even more serious consequences. On the other hand, apology is actually a form of release. It will allow both parties to see their true selves and break though the fairytale fantasies of how they previously viewed each other, thus allowing them to become closer to each other's true self.

Someone asked me, "What if I tried to apologize but the other party rejects my apology and refuses to forgive me?"

The person who apologizes cannot expect the other party's forgiveness. That is their freedom and their choice. An expectation that the other party definitely has to forgive them is just a way of trying to push the responsibility over to the other party. An apology should only be a show of our respect to the other party. The guilt should still belong to us and we should continue to carry it as we continue to find better ways to treat each other till we manage to find a balance within the relationship again. So the main issue is: how do we deal with our guilt? Do we cut it off or do we tell ourselves, "I am willing to carry the burden of this guilt,"? Carrying the guilt does not make us innocent. But carrying this guilt will give us strength and many good things can arise from this strength. If we do this, we will become humbler and more loving. This, in itself, is a type of powerful, new balance.

The Fluid Principle Of Balance

"Balance" is inherent in the principles of nature. And it is man's innate nature to be in balance. If someone is good to us, we will naturally reciprocate. If someone treats us badly, we won't feel like treating them well too. Therefore, if we are constantly in imbalance, our innate nature will start to take over and try to move towards a new balance. And this characteristic is especially evident in the relationship between men and women. But men and women have so many differences. Just how do they achieve balance? The Chinese symbol of Taijitu (太極圖, also known as the Yin Yang Symbol) has already given us the answer. The symbol shows the forces of Yin and Yang as a dynamic curve depicting equilibrium and not an equal, straight line. Also, within the 'Yin' there is a dot of 'Yang' and within the 'Yang', there is a dot of 'Yin'. Therefore, everyone has a bit of Yin and Yang energy within them. The crux of the interaction between the Yin and Yang is not in a sort of fixed, unchanging balance but a **flexible, fluid balance**.

In that case, how do we achieve a fluid balance between the two sexes? Through observations made from Bert Hellinger's insights (Hellinger, 2001e) and the countless cases I have facilitated, we discovered the secret behind the balance between the two sexes: **For positive returns, give back a little more; when it comes to negative returns, give back a little less**.

There are two types of balances between the two sexes. The first type is a Positive Balance. This means that when the other party is "good" to us, we will naturally want to return this goodness to them and treat them well. But in addition to that, this secret teaches us that when we are "paying back" the goodwill, we should pay back a little extra. This means that if the other party does something good for us that is worth 3 points (out of a scale of 10), when we return this goodwill, we should do something worth 5 points at least. The other party will feel happy that we have returned this much of goodwill and due to mankind's instinct to balance, they will want to treat us even better too.

And when we return this "better" kindness, we return it with just a little bit more too. The act of giving, receiving, returning more, giving, receiving and returning more repeats itself and this feeling of goodwill will become stronger. This positive interaction between the man and woman will continue to grow and from it, we will experience immense happiness and bliss.

Another type of balance is the balanced based on negative treatment of each other. This is one of the most important aspects of the interactions between the two sexes. However, many couples have not learnt how to work out the negative balance. This is especially so in Asian societies where tolerance is promoted and in Christian family's forgiveness is being promoted. But we have discovered in the tens and thousands of cases that we have processed, that when one party is not good to the other party and the other party were to either suppress their emotions or "pretend" to forgive the Perpetrator instead of really forgiving them, this will result in a vicious cycle. When their suppressed emotions finally do erupt, it will usually take the form of some sort of uncontrollable extreme behavior. News of violent crimes, suicides or murders are rather commonplace. In some cases, the parent even kills themselves together with their children, thus we can see that violence or an extreme form of revenge is not really a good way to restore balance.

Another situation that might arise is that some couples do not like to express or face up to the problems they have with their other half. Instead, they unconsciously make use of their children to control or harm them, thus making the innocent children suffer even more, even to the extent of affecting their marriages when they grow up. In this way, the unhappiness of the previous generation gets passed on to the next generation.

Let us investigate what is the best way to balance things out when both parties in a relationship hits a negative spot. The secret lies in this: when the other party treats us badly, we have to return the negativity. However, it is worthy to take note that your "returns" has got to be in a smaller amount than what you received. This means that if the other party does something bad to us that hits a 5 pointer (on a scale of badness from 0 to 10), whatever we do in return to them can only hit the 3 point mark. So at this point, even though the other party received 3 points worth of negativity, they are also receiving 2 points of goodwill from us. Thus, the relationship will not be filled with only negative emotions. Even if we were to get into a conflict again, our innate need for balance will exert an unconscious pressure to move towards a balance. As the 3 points of negativity being returned is also made better by 2 points of goodness, after adding a positive value of 2 to the negative 3, only 1 point of negativity is left. So when the other tries to balance this out, they will only return us 1 point worth of negativity. When we return that 1 point worth of negativity, we return less than a point's worth and eventually, we will either arrive at two possible conclusions: either to just forget it or to truly forgive. When we do this, the vicious cycle arising from negativity will eventually reduce. In replacement, there will instead be a teeny-weeny bit of positive cycle.

So, what is this "little bit" that we give more of and the "little bit" that we return less of?

That little bit is called **LOVE**.

Therefore, we should always return any form of negative treatment occurring within a relationship. However, it is important to remember that whenever we return it, we also return it with a "little bit of love". When we do this, we will be able to truthfully express our emotions while giving value to our relationship. Therefore, in order to have an excellent relationship, one must understand the Principle of Balance. A point to note though is that when we are good to other people, we must never keep thinking about how they should repay us for our goodness. Instead, please give naturally without any underlying conditions.

The instinct we have to achieve balance at all times can crate a rolling snowball of happiness. But it can also bring about devastating revenge from one's partner. A wise person who understands the Principle of Balance and uses it wisely will be able to bring abundance, happiness and ease into their lives and the lives of the people around them. That is because he or she will be able to create a loop of recurrent love.

Such a form of love supports the love energy in our lives. Therefore, our lives will support this love too.

Revenge And Reconciliation

Mahr (1998) summed up a good insight that is when a devastating revenge takes place in a relationship, one party will bring both themselves and their partners towards a common destruction. This is a terrorist-like behavior. This kind of revenge doesn't just ruin the other party but ruins us too. Not only do we increase the pain that we are experiencing, our future generations will also never be able to achieve reconciliation within their hearts. So, what is a better way to "revenge" on your partner when they cheat on you? From the Principle of Balance that I have just described, we have learnt that when we take revenge on the other party, relatively speaking, we give back a little less negativity than what they have given us. And this little bit of negativity we do not return is actually a form of love we have for that person. When we do this, we give ourselves a freedom to exit. Through this exit, we will be able to find new strength and power that will allow us to lead better lives. When the other party sees us walking out from our hurt and pain, it means they cannot really harm us. On the contrary, we have made use of this pain and anguish to move forward to a new level in our lives, achieving a brand-new level, which would not have been possible without this incident. In actual fact, only anger can be transformed into love. Just like two sides of the same coin, when you flip anger over, the other side is always love. This is a huge source of creative energy. Therefore, the best way to "pay back" would be to let ourselves lead even better lives. Only then, can we truly have peace and reconciliation within our hearts.

What is reconciliation? As Bert Hellinger says: "Reconciliation has got real power and value in it. Merely forgiving doesn't. It means we are allowing ourselves to have a brand-new start and part of this brand new start would be to agree to never ever go back to the past that we have left behind us. It is as if we have died yesterday and is given a new chance to be reborn again. This is true reconciliation."

Exercise: Applying the Principle Of Balance In A Relationship

Through the above mentioned story, we can see that when love is given without wisdom, it will never be able to grow and mature. If a couple in a relationship is not able to learn how to interact with balance, they will never be able to achieve true happiness.

Some may doubt if the innate Principle Of Balance really exists and operates within a relationship.

Let me invite you to experience this "Principle of Balance" yourself.

Please conduct an experiment on your other half but do not tell him what you are doing. Starting from today, within the next week, please apply the Principle of Balance on him/her every day. This means that if he/she is good to you, you will treat them better. If he/she is not good to you, you will repay it back with a little less negativity.

For example, if your partner does you a favor. Then, you will do them a slightly bigger favor. If your partner buys you a small present, you buy him/her something slightly better. If they kiss you once, you kiss them back twice. This "little bit more" that you return to them doesn't have to be substantial but it has to be given with love.

Remember that you have to do this secretly and should not tell the other party about your experiment. Neither should you expect any returns from your partner. If you really do apply this principle, in less than a week, your partner will definitely feel a difference and exclaim, "You seem to have changed!" Even so, please continue our experiment in secret and do not tell your partner about it. After some time, you will actually find that your relationship with each other has moved closer towards a healthier and happier direction.

In addition, the bigger benefit of this is that your partner will naturally want to balance things out and thus will be unknowingly influenced by you. And so, the two of you will have a chance to accumulate an abundant sense of happiness!

Abortion, The Pain And Heartache

Principle of Order: Everyone needs to have a place within the family system. This is true even for aborted fetuses (Hellinger et al., 1998).

Feng Zhi from Taipei is 45 this year. She is a business development manager of a popular high end restaurant franchise. A dynamic woman, this superwoman helped her company start umpteen branches within a very short time. Almost like the undefeatable Transformer robot, Feng Zhi doesn't (need to) rest when she works. When I met her at our workshop, she looked and behaved just like a robot. Her body was rigid and she never smiled. When I asked her what happened to her, she said that that she has not been speaking to her husband for many years. Even though they both lived in the same house, they rarely communicated with each other.

"I don't know why. It seems as if our characters clash with each other. Every time we try to talk to each other, we end up quarrelling. In the end, we become even more distant from each other. That is the reason why I put all my focus on my job. But I still continue to have a feeling of emptiness in my heart," Feng Zhi said.

"Perhaps the issue between the two of you is not what it seems on the surface. Do you still love your husband?" I asked her.

This questioned seemed to make an impact on her. She couldn't help but ask, "Do I still love him? We have been married for 20 years. Back then, I married him because I felt he was a decent, honest chap. We have been through so many challenges in the past 20 years and now, our children are all grown up. But, do I still love him?"

She paused to give this question a thought. After a while, she nodded her head and said, "Yes, I still love my husband."

"Does he still love you?"

This question sent a little tremor into her heart. After a short pause, she replied, "I guess he still loves me."

"So the both of you love each other but yet find it hard to live together."

"Yes, and this is the reason I am here in this workshop today."

"Good, now let us explore the real relationship between the both of you. Please choose two workshop participants whom you do not know. One of them will represent you. The other one will represent your husband."

Feng Zhi followed my instructions and chose two participants to represent herself and her husband.

"Based on how your heart perceives your relationship with your husband, place these two people inside the classroom to show the relationship between you and your husband." I continued to remind her, "When you are placing them, just clear your mind and just follow your intuition about where to place them."

Without any interruptions from others, Feng Zhi placed her and her husband very far away from each other. They were at least 5 meters apart.

"Look at how you have placed them. This is a manifestation of how far apart the both of you are in your sub conscious mind."

Feng Zhi kept quiet and bit her lip.

Following that, something interesting happened. The person representing Feng Zhi kept looking downwards at the floor in the middle of the room. Her eyes were glazed over and she looked like a zombie. And the person representing her husband was facing outwards. The both of them were not looking at each other at all.

"Can you see it? You keep looking down at the floor. We don't know what you are looking at. And your husband seems to be avoiding something. The both of you are avoiding something in your life."

I made an observation about her posture and continued to ask her, "Did you and your husband ever had an abortion?"

The word "abortion" acted like an electric current that flowed straight to the deepest pain in Feng Zhi's heart. She recalled that in the past few years, the times that they spoke to each other had been decreasing but yet the number of times they have aborted away their children…

"We aborted 11 children…" Feng Zhi's voice started to choke. Her eyes turned red and her face turned pale. She kept rubbing her hands together and she continued, "I ever watched Bert Hellinger's DVD. One of the ladies in the DVD said that she had 7 aborted children and Hellinger told her to lose all hope of being saved… I have 11 aborted children; I wonder if I can still be saved." Feng Zhi started to tear and tremble violently.

I held her hand firmly and looked deeply into her eyes. "Whether you can be saved does not depend on other people. It depends on you. Even the best experts can only help you along. The key to this is YOU. Do you understand?"

Feng Zhi stopped crying and she seems somewhat enlightened as she nodded her head.

After a while, I asked her, "Are you ready to face this issue?"

She kept quiet and made no response.

I stood by her side silently. After a while, she looked up, eyes red, voice shivering, she gave an affirmative, "Yes!"

I then invited 11 participants to represent the 11 aborted children. I got them to sit down on the floor in between the representative of Feng Zhi and her husband. "Now, please take a close look at your 11 children, just like a mother would."

Feng Zhi was flooded with tears and she started to wail. She kneeled down and hugged every single aborted child. Feeling the deep love and guilt she has towards them; she touched the faces of each child. Tears kept flowing down her face. Some of the children longed for her touch and hugged her tightly while crying; some of the children turned their heads away in anger. Some of them were peaceful, some of them felt lost. Some of them were sad, some of them were angry. Every child reacted differently to her touch. Feng Zhi continued to hug and stroke each and every one of them.

I asked her to speak to them and I guided her along. "I am your mother. We killed you. We will bear our responsibility and our guilt. You are free." Feng Zhi repeated these words sincerely from her heart. Everyone present was deeply touched. We saw that Feng Zhi's heart is starting to open up and she started to change…

After about half an hour, Feng Zhi started to feel more at peace and the children started to feel more at peace too.

"Now, one by one, give each of these children a place in your heart," I said.

Feng Zhi stood up and looked at every one of her children with the loving gaze of a mother. At this moment, something miraculous happened. The person representing Feng Zhi's husband started to turn his head over to look at them. This is the first time they looked at each other since the constellation process started.

Then, Feng Zhi spoke to the person representing her husband, "Let's face this issue together, shall we?"

He nodded his head and the two of them started to move closer to each other. Eventually, he moved right next to Feng Zhi and faced all their children together with her.

Feng Zhi's courage saved her and saved her marriage.

We ended the constellation there.

Feng Zhi asked me, "What else do I need to do after this when I go home?"

I replied, "Your heart is already starting to change. When you are back, don't be in a hurry to do anything. Let this whole process ferment slowly in your heart. When you are not forced to do anything but take things at its own natural course, the desire to do something will come from a strong surge of energy from your heart. When that happens, you can sit down and talk to your husband about how you feel about all these abortions. Then sincerely do some good deeds together in memory of your children."

Feng Zhi nodded her head.

I turned around and shared the following with the whole class. "Children are the crystallization of their parent's love. When a couple destroys the crystallization of their love, it is as good as them choosing to cut their relationship into half. It will cause a break in their bonding. Only when both parties are willing to bear responsibility for this together, will they have a chance to restart their relationship again."

A few months later, I met Feng Zhi at another one of my workshops. She had become a completely different person. She looked alive and happy. Her cheeks were rosy and there was a smile on her face. What is even more shocking is that she brought her husband along with her to the workshop.

"This is something I wouldn't be able to even dream of in the past! My husband used to oppose whenever I mentioned that I was going for a workshop. But since the last workshop, he noticed that there was a huge change in me and we conversed extensively about the abortions. That is why when I invited him to attend this workshop with me, he agreed. I feel it is such a miracle and I am so happy!" Feng Zhi smiled as she shared with the whole class.

Two years later, I happened to be having a business appointment near the Taipei Main Station. I remembered that someone told me that Feng Zhi had opened a restaurant selling healthy cuisine nearby. At that moment, I looked up and I found myself right in front of a restaurant. So I went in to take a look, thinking that there might be a chance I can see her there. The moment I stepped into the door; I saw Feng Zhi *making fruit juice behind the counter. She was so surprised to see me and warmly invited me to sit down for a juice as we caught up with each other. "After that, I quit my job and rested for a while. In the end, I decided to start a business and run it the way I like. I am no longer a workaholic who works nonstop. Now, I work at my own pace."*

Just as we were chatting happily, someone walked out from the kitchen. Make a guess who it was!

It was her husband! I was so pleasantly surprised!

Feng Zhi gave a brilliant grin and said, "After the last workshop, we started to communicate more and our relationship improved by leaps and bounds. When I said I wanted to start a shop, he volunteered to help out here."

Smiling, her husband passed me a bowl of soup and said, "Teacher Chou, how have you been? This is our signature dish- green bean barley soup. Our treat!"

The Effect Of Abortion On Both Partners

Feng Zhi initially thought that the issue between her and her husband was incompatibility and poor communication with each other. But through our deep exploration, we discovered that the root of the issue was that they were unwilling to acknowledge their aborted children. Neither of them was willing to face up to the truth of the matter and take up responsibility. This destroyed the intimate relationship between them and affected both their physical and mental health. "Abortion" may be a taboo topic for most couples. But it is a result stemming from a couple's most intimate interaction. Therefore, let us take a moment to explore "abortion" and the effects it has on a relationship.

The communion of husband and wife is like Yue Lao's (月佬, a Chinese deity in charge of marriages) red thread running through husband and wife and children are an extension of this red thread. Should a couple make a decision to remove the fetus unnaturally, it is equivalent to one taking a knife to chop the red thread into two. Therefore, the relationship between husband and wife will break down (Hellinger, 2001a).

After the abortion, it is impossible to pretend that nothing has happened and lie to ourselves; therefore, the relationship between the couple is no longer innocent. If the couple is not married, 90% of the time, they will break up after the abortion. If they are already married, the abortion will often lead to extramarital affairs, divorce, unexplainable quarrels, distancing between the couple. Sometimes they continue to pretend to close but are in actual fact distant. Or they may lead separate lives. From this, we can see that abortion is rather damaging to a relationship.

In addition, an abortion creates negative impact on both their physical and emotional health. For the woman, an abortion is just like cutting out a piece of her heart. Now that she has a hole in her heart, she will start to feel empty and depressed. Some of them may close down part of their emotional faculties and not feel altogether. In our example, Feng Zhi's unconscious strategy to make up for this is to put all her energies into her work so that she does not have to feel (the deep pain of losing a part of her heart). But the strategy was not a successful it. Putting her energies into work could not fill up that hole in her heart. Just like each individual piece in a jigsaw puzzle will have its rightful position and nothing else can replace it, the hole in Feng Zhi's heart is a place that belongs to her aborted children. It is only when she plucked up the courage to face the facts and admit to her own wrongdoings that she could give this place in her heart to her children. As the children took on their rightful place in her heart, the hole is mended. At the same time, Feng Zhi and her husband started to share about the emotions they had towards this incident and together, they did many good deeds in memory of their children. This is the only way that husband and wife can start anew wholeheartedly.

How Should Partners Face Abortion

As the Chinese saying goes, "A hundred years of spiritual cultivation together gives us the chance to be on the same boat, a thousand years of spiritual cultivation together will give us the chance to sleep on the same bed". In order to become husband and wife, it requires 1000 years of hard work. Therefore, it is an even more precious affinity that our children get to be born as our offspring. Should we have an abortion, how should we make this broken affinity whole again?

The first and foremost would be for both husband and wife to face it together and take up all the responsibilities together Hellinger (2001e).

I would like to emphasize that they keyword here is 'together'. And that is not the same as having one parent so upset that they try send the child away through some religious ritual, believing that their aborted fetuses are baby spirits who should be removed or chased off. All these are misguided concepts and they will not help the couple and the child achieve true reconciliation.

Think about it. Should this child be given a chance to be born, he or she will be our child and we would never do anything except love him/her. Then why should we think that they are no good or bad after we kill them? The only reason we have this sort of thinking is because we do not want to face up to our guilt. If we are unwilling to be responsible for what we have done, the husband-and-wife relationship will definitely start to show signs of crisis. The situation has a chance to change only when the couple is willing to face this incident together.

Secondly, husband and wife should vocalize how they each feel about abortion and share the sadness that they have Hellinger (2001e).

It is very important for the couple to vocalize what they feel about the abortion. For example, one could say, "Sometimes I would still think about this incident and it always makes me feel sad," or "I have always been feeling guilty about it, I don't know what I should do to make it better."

By giving our other half a chance to start to really understand how we feel, we, too, find a healthy way to face ourselves. Sharing our emotions will also help improve our relationship. When both parties start to interact and share about their sadness and guilt and discuss how they can bear this responsibility together, there will be a chance to mend the broken bonds between husband and wife and there is even a possibility that their relationship from then on will get even better.

If you have already broken up with your partner, what do you do about the children you have aborted? In actual fact, there is no difference in the situation as compared to a couple who are still together. This child is you and your ex-partner's child. Even though you may not have a chance to face it together and even if your relationship with that partner has ended, you still give the child a place in your heart. Just doing so will bring about a feeling of completion for the child and also for us and our bodies and hearts.

Thirdly, do better on behalf of your child and give your child a place in both your hearts Hellinger (2001e).

How do we give this child a place in our hearts? Some examples of what people do would be to grow a tree on behalf of the child. Or we could do something memorable; we could buy them gifts on special occasions and treat them like normal children. Should the couple is go on a trip, they could also say in their hearts, "Dad and mum will bring you out and have fun together.", "This is where dad and mum met,", "This is where we put you into mummy's tummy,", etc. And you can do more good deeds on their behalf. For example, you can donate money to help the children from the poorer third world countries or volunteer in an orphanage. You may even wish to bring your partner along and tell the child in your heart, "Dad and Mum are doing this for you." Alternatively, you can choose to bring blessing or salvation to them by performing certain religious rituals. In short, our aim is to let these children feel happiness and peace through these healthful methods. By giving them our blessings and doing many good deeds on their behalf, we will love them like how a father or mother should. And please remember, the point of the whole exercise is not how you do it but the extent of your sincerity.

The Effect Of Abortion On Men

Because an abortion is an operation that takes place on a woman's body, we very often neglect the effect it has on men. There is a study in America about how abortion affects men. They discovered that while the abortion has no physical effect on men, emotionally, the effect of an abortion on man is in fact the same as a woman. Men will also develop guilt, feel depressed, close up their hearts and feel emptiness. It is just that men are generally weaker at expressing their emotions and not so good and verbalizing them. But men will express these emotions in a different way (Schelotto & Arcuri 1986).

For example, in my work, I have often noticed that men will unconsciously use their careers, religion, alcohol, money or material things to try and fill up the void they feel inside. Some men even use failure as a form of compensation to deal with the guilt arising from the abortion. They unconsciously fill their career with challenges and pitfalls so that they will not be able to enjoy the true success and wealth. Why would that be? This is because all the external achievements are unable to fill the void that they have in their hearts. Unless we are willing to give this child a place in our hearts to fill up the void, we will never be able to feel free and cheerful.

The Effect Of Abortion On Our Children

An abortion may affect our children who are living. It may affect the trust between parent and child and the child may even feel some feelings of abandonment. As a result, they may become distant and distrust their parents. In more serious cases, they might identify with their dead sibling and thus fall sick easily or refuse to eat (Hellinger et at., 1998).

However, if we approach our aborted children with a healthy mindset, it will be very helpful for our children who are still alive. Because the living children now know that their parents will be responsible for their actions. Not only will the child learn to be accountable, when a parent is willing to give all their children- regardless of what has happened- a place in their heart, the child will experience a special sense of stability. The parent does not need to share all the details with the living children. They key lies not in whether these children know about all the minute details about their aborted siblings but in the **attitudes** of the parents. For example, when we are sharing about the abortion with our children, we have to let them feel that both parents really have a place in their hearts for these aborted children. In this way, the children will be able to feel their parent's love. This is a more suitable approach. On the other hand, if the parents do not feel any love for the aborted child, and have not given them a place in their hearts, or perhaps they are telling their children about this out of their own guilt as they want their kid to help them bear the burden of the guilt, then, it is not really a good idea to tell the child.

When we love and develop a healthy attitude towards the aborted child, the children who are alive will unconsciously feel free. That is because the child will no longer need to feel guilty, lonely or angry about being the one who is alive. They will also have no need to fear that their parents might abandon them like how they abandoned their aborted siblings. Therefore, they can return to their rightful place amongst the siblings.

How To Communicate With Your Other Half

Sometimes, our partner may not be willing to touch on this subject because of the guilt they feel. Perhaps they do not know how to face up to the abortion, therefore, they may choose to seal up their emotions or give themselves logical explanations to neglect the mistake they have committed. At this moment, we have to open ourselves up and vocalize our emotions and thoughts on the abortion. That doesn't mean we start to argue about the size of the child or whether they have got life, because all these are just defense mechanisms of the brain. What we have to do is to sincerely let the other party know how we feel and we can ask them, "Have you ever felt sad about this before?", "I would like to make myself feel better. Shall we do some good deeds for our child together?"

We do not have to force the other party to do anything. According to my experience, when the wife and husband start to discuss this issue, they will get a chance to communicate and talk about their emotions and when they do that, they move a step closer and start to really see each other. This is the only way they can build a new relationship. When we adopt a healthy attitude towards the issue of abortion, even if we should feel guilt, it is a healthy form of guilt. Therefore, the key lies in our attitude towards abortion. Did we communicate deeply from our hearts? If the answer is no, then we will have to keep paying the price until we learn our lesson.

At the same time, please remember that all feelings of guilt will come to an end one day. After we face the situation courageously, we must find a suitable time to end the guilt. Some people take 5 years, some 8. Some even longer. The time it takes may differ for everybody. But eventually, we have to let the guilt go if we want this child to truly rest in peace.

Inner Constellations Exercise: Praying For Your Aborted Child

It is indeed a rare and precious affinity for a child to come into our body. There should be value in the deaths of these children. We have to learn the important lesson from the huge sacrifice our children have made. We have to lead even better lives because this is the best form of respect for the departed children.

There is a Systemic Constellations Exercise that you can process in your heart. I call it "Inner Constellations". As long as we focus, go back to our center and are able to visualize and self-direct, the effect of an Inner Constellation is actually the same as you getting someone else to represent you in a normal constellation. Now, I would like to invite you walk through the process of an Inner Constellation together. Let's pray for all aborted children, first, let's pray for your own aborted children. If you have never aborted any children, then please pray for your siblings or family members within your family system who may have been aborted. Pray for their happiness and peace.

Let us raise ourselves, raise ourselves
Raise ourselves higher, higher, and onto a higher realm

In that place, everyone is loved
All the children in that place are totally accepted
We have arrived in this higher realm
In front of us we see
All the unfortunate children in our family who have been aborted
Fill your gaze with love, look at them with love
Regardless of whether they are our children
Our siblings
These unfortunate children in our family
Take a good look at them
They are unable to live on like us
Let us gaze at them with love
Let us see these children
Now say to them
"Dear children
Now I can see all of you
We have killed all of you
We are willing to take up the responsibility and guilt
You are free
Even though the time you spent in this family is short
But you are a part of our family
Now, I will give every one of you a place in my heart
It is a pity you did not get to live on
But we are still living on
We have benefitted from your deaths
The sacrifice you made will not be without value
I will let my future be even brighter and become even more successful
I will share my success with you, my happiness
Share with you the peace in my heart
Please bless me
Should I have my own children
Should my children live on healthily
Please protect them like angels
Dear children
Now, I leave my love for you
Blessing you such that no matter where you will be
You can always feel peace and joy
Now allow yourself to look further, look further
Look beyond these children

See the higher and further places behind them
That is the source of life
Imagine that there is limitless, bright, golden light there
Golden light, white light
Filled with blessings, filled with happiness
That is the source of life
We look at our children
As they start to walk towards the source of life
And return to the source of their lives
Bringing along with them our blessings
Going back to this golden, white light
Dear children, I bless all of you
Dear children, please leave in peace
Wave to them or give them a bow
Happily send them on their journey
See them melt into this golden, white light
The light of the source of life
Then, we bring with us this peace, this joy
And return to the present

After we finish this Inner Constellations Exercise, we can do something good for the children in our society who might need help. This is an elevation of our lives. Our love now has a definite direction to flow towards. It is flowing towards ourselves, our children, our family and flowing in a direction that benefits our society.

Weddings, Hindrance Or Support From Our Families

A marriage does not only take place between two persons. It is actually the coming together of two families. If the couple respects each other's family, their families will become a form of support towards their relationship and their marriage will be one filled with happiness (Hellinger, 2001a).

Shou Yi is a very outstanding man. However, he has a very unique, independent line of thinking and is thus often thought of as an oddity. He was a Masters Student in a famous school but he quit school because he said he was looking for the real truth of life. Through his searches, he has gone through many different types of spiritual cultivation practices and personal improvement courses and by the time he came to me, he was almost 40 years old.
"Have you found the truth you are looking for?"
"No, but I would like to find a girlfriend."
"Oh, congratulations! You are one step closer to the truth!" I teased him with a smile.
Shou Yi looked a little shy.
"It's true. I am not kidding you. Socrates is a good example."

He touched his head in embarrassment, "I had a few girlfriends but our relationships never last long. I would like to have a long term relationship."
I stopped the teasing and told him, "Very well, let us explore what is obstructing you from having this."
I asked Shou Yi to stand up and choose someone to represent the girl whom he will have to affinity with in the future and got him to stand in front of her. When Shou Yi was facing the representative, it was obvious that he lacked confidence. He shuffled around on the spot and seemed fearful of moving closer. Because of that, the representative representing his potential true love started to shrink backwards too.
"Hmm, there is not enough masculine energy in your ancestral line," I commented and I asked him, "Did anything special happen to the male ancestors in your family? Did anything happen to your father, your grandfather or even your great grandfather?"

Shou Yi replied, "Mmm.. My grandfather and great grandfather passed away when they were very young. As for my maternal great grandfather, I am not really sure. We seldom talk about him at home."
I got a few representatives to represent Shou Yi's grandfather, great grandfather and maternal great grandfather and included them into the constellations. When they moved into their positions, something strange happened. When Shou Yi saw them, for some unknown reason, he started to kneel down and cry. He was very agitated. Those were not tears of sadness but the tears of immense joy of someone who finally found something or someone that they were looking for.
"Perhaps, this is the truth that you have been searching for!" I said.
When he finished shedding his tears of joy, I got Shou Yi's father, grandfather, great grandfather, maternal grandfather, maternal great grandfather and even his great, great grandfather to stand behind Shou Yi. This group of male ancestors was like life's legacy being passed down from one generation to another. With the support all his male ancestors, Shou Ye started to feel the legacy of life and its power behind him. He found the power to be a real man. He started to stand straight and pushed his chest out and he started to move slowly towards the girl in front of him. At this moment, his potential true love was also willing to come closer.
I reminded him, "Remember this power, and remember the power of the generations of fathers behind you. You must remember this feeling forever. In future when you meet the girl of your dreams, remember this power behind you and move towards her. Can you remember to do that?"
Shou Yi nodded his head resolutely.
A year later, Shou Yi brought Zi Xuan to my workshop. Zi Xuan was a graceful and gentle-looking girl. She was in fact the belle of the army and an expert in Judo and self-defense martial arts. Shou Yi says that they have been dating for a little more than 6 months and they love each other very much. They wanted to get married but Zi Xuan's mother was strongly against the idea. They tried their best to persuade her but no matter what they did or said, she refused to approve of their marriage.
"My mum even said that if we really do get married, she will refuse to attend our wedding!" Zi Xuan's eyes were red from crying.
"Okay, let us explore and see how we can complete this affinity," I replied.

I invited a few people to represent Shou Yi, Zi Xuan and Zi Xuan's mother. When Zi Xuan's mother was added into the constellations, she kept looking afar and walking towards that direction.
I asked Zi Xuan, "What do you know about the situation in your mum's family?"
She replied, *"My mum and dad are divorced. My grandma and my grandfather are also not on good terms."*
"It seems that the marriages in the last two generations of your family did not go too well."
"Yes."
I added in a few representatives to represent Zi Xuan's father, maternal grandfather and grandmother into the constellations. Soon, we observed that her grandmother was very angry with her grandfather and so she was standing very far away from the family. We also observed that Zi Xuan's mother never once looked at her husband. She was just walking towards the grandma who was standing far away from the family. Eventually, she walked right next to grandma, kneeled down and held on to her leg.
I looked at the constellations and said, "I now know why your mother does not approve of this marriage."
Zi Xuan nodded her head, *"Since young, my mum has never received much love from my grandmother. My grandmother was suffering very much."*
"Yes, your mother loves your grandmother very much, so much that she even wanted to leave this family together with your grandmother. And your mother's divorce with your father is also her way of showing her loyalty to your grandmother."
Next, *I asked Zi Xuan to bow deeply to her mother and grandmother. Then I asked her to tell them, "I can see your fates. I know you have suffered in your marriages and I know it is not easy to be a wife. But I will try my best and I would like your blessings. Should my marriage turn out differently, should I be able to own my happiness, that will be my way of loving you. Please bless me."*
With tears in her eyes, Zi Xuan repeated those words. Her mother and grandmother started to hug her and the three generations cried together in tight embrace.
And indeed, should the female ancestors in your family system have a sense of distrust towards marriage and have ever been treated unfairly in their marriage, then the future female offspring of the family will

often try to show their loyalty to these ancestors by taking on the same emotions and even having the same situation happening in their marriages.

When the three of them stopped crying, I invited Shou Yi to give Zi Xuan's parents a bow and got him to promise that he will definitely take good care of Zi Xuan. But Zi Xuan's mother did not even glance at him and just continued to hug Zi Xuan tightly.

The constellations got stuck in this situation for a long time. After spending more time on the process, nothing seemed to be moving forward. Just as I was about to give up hope, I was hit by a sudden inspiration.

"It looks like this marriage needs some sort of support energy." I said. I added Shou Yi's parents into the constellations and asked them to be friendly towards Zi Xuan's mother, grandmother, uncle and the rest of the family, promising to take good care of their daughter-in-law. In the end, Zi Xuan's uncle was the first person to accept Shou Yi. Zi Xuan's mother was influenced by this and eventually, she managed to accept this son-in-law.

Even though in actual fact, only Shou Yi and Zi Xuan were present at the constellations, I asked them to put the whole process in their hearts.

"The path towards this marriage requires a little bit of hard work but fortunately, you now know which direction you should be working towards," I encouraged them and turned to Shou Yi, "You need to do your best to proof that Zi Xuan will be happy with you. Only then will Zi Xuan's family trust you. At the same time, remember that your parents will be one of your biggest supports and they will be the deciding factor that determines if the two of you will be able to get married!"

I then turned to Zi Xuan and told her, "Even though your mother is sorely disappointed with her marriage and thus unable to trust men, but she still wishes for you to be happy."

Zi Xuan and Shou Yi nodded their heads gratefully.

Another year has passed and I received a wedding invite from Shou Yi and Zi Xuan. They insisted that I definitely have to attend their wedding and even gave me a seat in the VIP table that is reserved for the bride, groom and their parents. I happily agreed. When I arrived there, what made me even happier was that I saw Zi Xuan's mother *was at the wedding. Even though Zi Xuan's mother looked very petite, you could tell that she has been through a lot in life and I could see the strength in her eyes. I saw Shou Yi's mother holding on warmly to her hand as they walked around to raise glasses with their family and friends. The band was playing joyous music and everybody was happy and joyful. A little more than a year later, I received a picture that Shou Yi and Zi Xuan sent to me. They have given birth to a baby girl. She looked very chubby and was really cute!*

"Your family can be a hindrance or a form of support. It all depends on whether we truly understand the Principles of Love." This is my greatest insight from their life story.

Conscience And The Loyalty of Love

"Loyalty" means that the children will do exactly as their parents or their family did.

If you observe a child for some time, you will notice that a child will often want to dress like their parents, eat the same foods, say the same words, and behave in the same way so as to show that they belong to the same team as their parents. We are not only referring to young children here but children in general to all parents. That is because even if we were to grow up, we would still hold on to this loyalty. When this sort of loyalty appears, we become children again.

This is a form of sub conscious longing. We thought that through the same behavior, we would be able to "continue bonding with our parents" and feel the sense of belonging that arises from "being on the same team". Hellinger (1998) terms this sort of subconscious phenomenon as "conscience". This sort of conscience stems from the love a child has for their family. But unfortunately, this sort of love is a form of blind love and not a form of mature love. That is because the children mistakenly think that as long as the same things happening to their parents are repeated in their own lives, they will be able to maintain this bond with their parents. Sometimes, to show their loyalty, they even make blind sacrifices for their families. But the children are not aware that this form of love will actually replicate the tragedies in their parent's lives in the future generations. For example, if the parents have a failed marriage, the child might unconsciously follow their parents and allow their marriage to fail miserably too. Just like the example we mentioned earlier, Zi Xuan, like her mother and her grandmother might then be suffering from a failed marriage just like them.

How do we break through such a repetitive destiny? The answer is that the child must find the courage to bear this guilt. Even if our parents had an unhappy marriage, we must also do our best to have a happy marriage.

To do this requires courage. That is because most children believe that if they do that, it will mean that they are being disloyal to their parents and their family. But the truth of the matter is quite the opposite. Regardless of what the child does, the bond between child and parent is a bond of life, a relationship that exists since our birth and it is undeniable. Even if we were to say that we want to cut off the relationship between us and our father or mother, the fact of the matter is that we are still their children and they are still our parents no matter what. This is a fact of life and it will never change.

If the child is able to understand this, they will be able to lead their lives to the fullest and use a form of mature love to repay their gratitude to their parents. There is nothing parents all over the world would like more than to see their children lead happy lives. Such is the wisdom of love.

Principle Of The Flow: Linking Up With The Male And Female Energy Of Our Ancestors

Hellinger (2001e) summarized his consulting experiences that when men are able to link up with the male power of their ancestors, they will become real men and will attract the opposite sex; likewise, when a woman can link up with the female energy of their ancestors, they will become an attractive, mature woman. "Opposites attract" and just like the attraction between the Yin and the Yang, the Positive and the Negative, the attraction between opposites is natural. From the real life example mentioned above, we can see that even though a person may want to have a long term relationship, but when his connection with the male energy of his ancestors is not there, he becomes a weak magnet and will not be able to attract other people who may want a long term relationship. But when he is linked up with the male power of his ancestors, he will start to look and behave like a man and become more confident. Suddenly, he will look more mature and more attractive to his potential long-term partner and she will be willing to move closer to him.

Should a man want to go into a long-term husband and wife relationship and transform himself from a boy into a man, and should he also want the respect and trust of women, the most important thing he has to do is to respect his father and link up with the male energy of the male ancestors. In that way, he will respect women and women will in turn respect and trust him. Only then will the women be willing to go into a long-erm husband and wife relationship with him.

In the same line of reasoning, just how can a girl transform herself into a woman? She needs to respect her mother and link up with the female energy of her ancestors. In this way, men will be able to trust her more and only then will she be able to attract men who are truly interested in being in a long term husband and wife relationship with her.

Therefore, when we are a "boy" or a "girl", it is possible for us to have many boyfriends or girlfriends and have many short-term relationships, but it would be difficult for us to build a long term husband and wife relationship unless we transform ourselves into "men" or "women". When that happens, long term relationships become possible. That is because when a boy links with the men in the family, he will no longer be a single boy but will also carry the energy from all the men in his family. That is like having a many powerful magnets stacked up behind him. This sort of attraction is the gift that life has given to men and women. At our end on the family tree, should we be able to link up and reach all the way back to the source of life, our hearts will be able to feel a deep stability and vastness that is deeply rooted to life. That is when we will be ready to move into a long-term relationship and be willing to service life together.

Inner Constellations Exercise: Linking Up With The Source Of Life

The Inner Constellations exercise that works on linking up with the source of life is a very good exercise. It is not only helpful for people who want to start long term relationships. When we feel like we are in need of more support or when we seem to have challenges in our careers, our jobs and our lives, it will also be very helpful. For this exercise, you may recite the following silently your heart or get another person to guide you along. Alternatively, you might wish to play the audio resource.

Please sit in an upright position

Let your feet touch the floor and feel the support from Mother Earth
Collecting and centering yourself
Imagine that your parents are standing behind you
Your father and your mother
Imagine how they look like
Behind your parents are their fathers and mothers
These are your grandfathers and grandmothers
Now you look further backwards
Behind them are their fathers and mothers
These are your great grandfathers and great grandmothers

Just like this
Every person has their father and mother standing behind them
One generation after another
You look further backwards at your forefathers, your ancestors
Every person has their father and mother standing behind them
Behind you are thousands of generations of ancestors
Continue looking backwards
Keep on looking backwards
You can feel that there are thousands of people standing behind you

Now trace further backwards
Continue to trace onwards
Trace all the way back to the source of life

You can imagine that as a limitless huge, bright light
A golden light, a white light
Beyond time and space, immensely bright
And beyond this bright light is absolute darkness, pure darkness
That is the source of life
You can imagine life linking up with this darkness
Through this light, moving into the hearts of the ancestors standing behind you
Life is thus passed down from one generation to another
Passing through your ancestors
Passing through your forefathers
Life as it is, not bigger or smaller
Passing down from one generation to the next
Passing down to your great grand parents
Your grand parents
Your father and mother
And lastly
Passing to you

Feel the light of life flowing into your heart
Feel the thousands of people standing behind you
The light of life flowing into their hearts
And eventually flowing into yours
Remember this picture
Remember

Chapter 3: Relationship With Our Parents

For you should know, and so I will explain: Even if a person carries his father on his left shoulder and his mother on his right shoulder, grinding his skin to bones, wearing the bones out to bone marrow by walking round Mountain Xu Mi, after hundreds and thousands of disasters that cut through flesh and make his blood flow, he will still be unable to repay the immense debt of gratitude he has towards his parents; Even if a person tries to overcome famine for his parents by using his body, grinding his body into pieces like tiny specks of dust, even after hundreds and thousands of such disasters, he will still be unable to repay the immense debt of gratitude he has towards his parents... Even if a person swallows a heated metal ball and goes through a thousand calamities and allows his body to become burnt and rotten, he will still be unable to repay the immense debt of gratitude he has towards his parents.
-- Buddha, Filial Piety Scripture

汝等當知,我今為汝分別解說:假使有人,左肩擔父,右肩擔母,研皮至骨,穿骨至髓,遶須彌山,經百千劫,血流沒踝,猶不能報父母深恩;假使有人,遭饑饉劫,為於爹娘,盡其己身,臠割碎壞,猶如微塵,經百千劫,猶不能報父母深恩…假使有人,為於爹娘,吞熱鐵丸,經百千劫,遍身焦爛,猶不能報父母深恩。

--佛陀《父母恩重難報經》

Life: The Most Precious Gift

When our parents give us life and allow us to come into this world, this is the best gift our parents can ever give to us. They have done all they could for life and allow life to be passed down onto earth. If our parents take good care of us, it is a bonus. Should the child not be able to see this precious gift and only see the things which he feels lacking in while thinking that his/her parents have not done enough or should do better, the child will end up disappointed and discontented. This will affect our entire lives. It will draw us into scarcity, depression and eventually, failure (Franke-Gricksch, 2003).

Indeed, some children may not be able to receive much love or care from their parents, but the child would still be able to receive this from other people like from their great grandparents, their grand parents, relatives or other care givers. If not, we wouldn't even be here. Therefore, in actual fact, whatever we have received is already "enough". When we keep harping on the love we never got and keep focusing on it, our hearts will become poorer because we will neglect all that we already have. At this moment, we create a black hole inside our hearts. Not only do we weaken our sense of happiness, even the bliss and happiness felt by the people around us will be sucked into this black hole.

So, what is this black hole? The black hole is the vacant position belonging to our parents in our hearts. When we do not give our parents a place in our hearts, we will feel a sense of emptiness; when we judge or go against our parents, we are also going against our own source of life. That means we are trying to make ourselves bigger than our parents and make it seem as if we have a more important position than they do. But all these will go against the "Principle Of Order".

Just like the enlightened being in India, Osho, once said, "Half of you comes from your father, half of you comes from your mother. Because of them, you are here; without them, there wouldn't be you.... You need to be aware of this." We may not agree with or like what our parents do, but if we denounce their positions just because of their behavior, it would be like us severing our ties with our roots. This will only give our hearts a even greater sense of emptiness and bring about a bigger disorder within the family.

On the other hand, we might also choose to become aware that our parents are the only ones who can give us the most precious gift of life. Because of this life, we are given a chance to learn, feel and experience so many wonderful things in life. Because of this life, we have the chance to grow and become enlightened. Even the great Shakyamuni Buddha exclaimed that "It is indeed difficult to repay the immense debt of gratitude towards our parents!"—Therefore, not only should we try to repay our parents with gratitude and see all the abundance that they have given us, we also have to also respect their positions as parents from our hearts. This is the only way our hearts can be filled with happiness because a person who counts his blessings is a truly happy person. When we can repay our debts towards our parents with deep gratitude, our hearts will find true peace (Franke-Gricksch, 2003).

The Truth Is: I Love You, Dad (Single Parent Families)

Our true happiness comes from respecting our parents as they truly are. Children who expect or wish for their parents to become something else will never be happy. That is why some people are perpetually griping over their grievances, day dreaming and they never grow up or become mature (Ulsamer, 2005).

Ah Xiong grew up in a single parent family. With the encouragement of his wife, he attended one of my workshops and his goal was to "get to know and understand myself". He even jokingly told us, "Because we have been quarrelling a lot lately, my wife says I am a schizophrenic! Ha ha..."

After making a joke out of himself, he started to share his story. "I am thirty this year and I used to be very introverted. To date, no one around me is able to understand me. My father had an affair and I really hate him..."

Even though he knew that his father ended the affair and committed suicide afterwards, Ah Xiong still used the word "hate" to describe his displeasure towards his father. However, the hearts of father and sons are still linked together and so Ah Xiong admitted that since his father's suicide, both him and his brother have been unable to forget it and he even contemplated suicide himself.

I asked him very seriously, "If you were to kill yourself, would it help the situation?"

He kept very quiet.

After a while, he couldn't contain his anger and said, "Then is his suicide helpful? He is totally irresponsible!"

I replied, "Yes, his suicide was not helpful. Likewise, would your suicide be helpful? In addition, would your children behave like you and feel the same way about it?"

"I am really conflicted and filled with contradiction. If not for my wife and my son, I really do not know what would have happened to me." Ah Xiong's words were filled with agitation and helplessness.

"Indeed, because your parents are in conflict, it is natural that you feel conflicted and feel as if you have two contradicting selves. But for the sake of yourself and your family, will you be willing to make good use of this chance and reintegrate these two conflicting parts? Are you willing to do that?"

Ah Xiong tried to nod his head but I know he is undergoing a huge battle within.

Following that, I invited two representatives to represent the two personalities within him. One of them is the personality of "the lonely heart" and the other is the personality of "the boy who is reliant on his mother". I also invited another four people to represent Ah Xiong's parents, wife and son and included them in the constellations.

When everyone was in position, we noticed that the two personalities are very far away from each other and looking at each other from afar just like how his parents were also standing very far apart. "The lonely heart" kept gazing at his father and seemed to have a desire to move closer towards the father. "The boy who is reliant on his mother" is constantly beside his mother. Ah Xiong's wife is standing by the side, hoping to get her husband's attention and his son was facing "the lonely heart".

"The two personalities within you are indeed separated. One of them wishes to follow your father and the other wishes to follow your mother." I told him.

Ah Xiong gritted his teeth and continue to look at the constellations with much concern.

I continued to ask him, "How does your mother talk about your father?"

"She hates him very much. She hates him for having an affair and always not being around. Since young, me and my mother have been dependent on each other. He was very mean to my mother and he was a very irresponsible man. I hate him too."

I pointed at the representatives inside the constellations, "Do you see? The two representatives who represent your two personalities are separated just like your parents. Even though on the surface, you kept criticizing your father, but one personality within you actually longs for your father and has already left this family like your father did. The other personality is very loyal to your mother, always keeping your mother company. If you are unable to come to a reconciliation with your parents, your son will end up like you. This sort of conflict that arises from parents who have separated will continue on and reappear in our future generations.

And indeed, the constellation has exposed what is currently happening. When we added Ah Xiong's two-year-old son into the constellation, he chose to be nearer to Ah Xiong's "the lonely heart" personality. And he kept looking back and forth between Ah Xiong's parents. This means that Ah Xiong's son is already being influenced by this information about the separation.

"When you are in such a conflicted family, all the children will be filled with conflict. And that includes you and your son. Are you ready to face your parent's relationship issue?"

For his son and for himself, Ah Xiong nodded his head resolutely.

I told him, "You have been embroiled into your father and mother's war. If you do not go back to your own position, your heart will always be conflicted."

"Then what should I do?"

"The first thing you have to do is to bid goodbye to your mother and take yourself out of the war between your father and mother."

With tears in his eyes, Ah Xiong repeated after me, "Mum, I know it has been very difficult for you, thank you for your care, thank you for all the sacrifices you have made for me..." He kneeled down in front of his mother and continued bravely, "I am so sorry I am unable to take over the anger you have towards dad. After all, I am still his son."

His mother started to hug him tightly and both of them embraced in tears.

"Mum, I have to go and look for dad now..."

When Ah Xiong said that, his dad who had died in regret during the suicide attempt was finally able to lie down in peace. It was as if a knot in his heart had finally been loosened after many years.

Ah Xiong walked to his father and honestly shared the anger in his heart. But he was choking when he said, "I was only willing to accept you when you committed suicide. Wah.... wah... wah..." he started bawling sadly.

After all, every child receives their gift of life from their parents. Even if they were to bear a huge grudge against their parents, the bonding and relationship between parent and child can never be cut into two.

Ah Xiong went on his knees and with tears in his eyes, he continued, "Daddy... Daddy... Daddy..."

I wonder how long he has been longing to call out to his father.

"Daddy... Daddy..."

He has not called out to his father for a long, long time.

"Daddy... Daddy..."

After some time, Ah Xiong started to calm down a little.

I guided Ah Xiong to say, "You are my only father. Please accept me as your son again."

"You are my only father. Please accept me as your son again," Ah Xiong repeated after me.

"Tell your father that you are married."

"Dad, I am already married and now I have a son too."

I continued to guide him, "If my marriage turns out to be different from yours, please bless me."

"If my marriage turns out to be different from yours, please bless me."

Ah Xiong kneeled down beside his dad and hugged him for a while. Despite the reunion after many years, they will have to bid farewell in death.

Ah Xiong said, "Dad, please rest in peace."

"I love you."

Ah Xiong said the last sentence very slowly and he was filled with love when he said that. The contradiction and conflict that existed within him started to melt away. In its place instead, was love, a very mature love.
Finally, "the boy who is reliant on his mother" kneeled down and "the lonely heart" started to move closer to each other… Eventually, these two personalities stood side by side and together, they moved closer towards his wife and son.

"Sometimes, reconciliation is only possible after death. But if we cannot even reconcile after death, it would be such a huge pity," I was inspired and touched.

Thankfully, no cause of regret happened in this instance because very shortly, right at the end of the constellation, both Ah Xiong and his son started to feel happy.

I am truly happy for them. Ah Xiong and his family can finally hug freely and bath in happiness, accepting all the joy and bliss that came with it. This is especially so for Ah Xiong. Because of his love for his mother, he got embroiled into his parents' fight. On one hand, he would like to help his mother by bearing all the anger and yet on the other hand, he longed to be closer to his father. Therefore, the two personalities within him separated as one of them wanted to continue to be dependent on his mother while the other wanted to be independent. This separation has affected his current family life and also affected his relationship with both his son and his wife. After so many years of suffering, for the sake of his wife and son and himself, he finally plucked up the courage to face the pain that is hiding in his heart so that he can find his position in the family again and reintegrate his two separated personalities.

Principle of Order: Transforming Blind Love Into Mature Love
When children see their parents quarrelling and getting separated, they feel immensely sad. So, these children think "I don't want to be like my parents in future!" But the strange thing is that even though their brain will tell them that and in order not to become like their parents, they will observe their parent's behavior in great detail. Because their observation is so detailed, they will remember it very well. When they finally find their own partners, however, they somehow always end up behaving exactly like their parents. Why is this so? The hidden motivation for that is the "loyalty" the children have for their parents.

This sort of "loyalty" is a common dynamic in systemic constellations. "I will follow you,", "I will do exactly as you do." Just like we mentioned previously, as long as we observe our children, we will understand what "loyalty" is. For example, the child will like to dress like his father or will want to eat the same foods as his mother. Through behaving in the same way, the child believes that they can keep the bonding and connection between parent and child and so, they will stick to the "we are on the same team" sort of thinking. But the idea of being "on the same team" will cause the child to repeat the destinies or patterns in their parent's lives (Franke, 2003a).

Consequently, if the parents have an unhappy marriage and the child desires to have a happy marriage, the child will certainly meet with challenges. Of course, this is not an impossible dream but how do we overcome this challenge? This will require lots of courage and wisdom. Firstly, the child has to respect the way his parents interact and take the courage to move back to his position as a child. When he is too close to his parents, he will easily be unconsciously embroiled into their fight and their problems. Therefore, it is important for the child to move back into their position of a child.

Secondly, the child has to demolish the idea that they will be able to maintain their bonding with their parent if they repeat whatever happens in their parents' lives. As a child, we have to make a firm decision and decide that even if our parents do not have happy marriages, we must also allow ourselves to be happy. This might be really difficult for some people because the child might feel as if they have betrayed their parents and feel a sense of guilt and fear that they might be disconnected with their parents. However, the opposite is true. When we make good use of the life our parents give us and let ourselves lead better lives, this will be the best way the child can show gratitude to their parents. Hellinger once said, "Guilt is the necessary price for growth." If the child can move through this guilt, they will be able to transform their blind love into a mature love and that is, "Even if I am happy and blessed, I will still be connected to my parents." (Hellinger et al.,1998).

No matter what the child has done, the blood relations between parent and child cannot be cut off. Even if they were to talk about cutting off their relationships with their parents, in actual fact, we are still their children and they are still our parents. This is a fact that will never change. If we can awaken based on this point, we will be able to lead our lives to the fullest and will allow ourselves to be happy and will be able to love and show filial piety to our parents with this mature love. And to our parents, this is what they would like to see most. Just like what Confucius said in the Book of Filial Piety, "Our bodies, including our hair and skin, are given to us by our parents, so we must not presume to injure or destroy them. This is the beginning of filial piety. When we live up to the TAO, we can leave a name and legacy for the future generations and thereby glorify our parents and make them happy, this is the consummation of filial piety." (身體發膚，受之父母，不敢毀傷，孝之始也；立身行道，揚名於後世，以顯父母，孝之終也。) When we are even happier, healthier and more successful than before, when we pass on the love that our parents have given us to the next generation, and use this life to do lots of good deeds and contribute to mankind, our parents will be proud of us. The inherent nature of filial piety will be brought to play and we will have a more satisfactory relationship with our parents.

I Am Sorry, Mum (Order and Body Size)

If our love goes against the Principle of The Order, this sort of love will not just cause disharmony in relationships but also affect our bodies and minds (Hellinger, 2003d).

Wang Juan from Xi An attended one of my workshops. She has a very big and bloated figure and is about thirty years old. It was very difficult not to notice her in the workshop because she weighed more than a hundred kilograms. Unlike the other participants, she will never give me a friendly nod of the head, nor will she chit chat with me or ask me any questions. She would just sit down with her friend in the position that is furthest away from me. During the workshop, she would be very serious. After it ends, she will keep within her group and speak to her friends and she doesn't interact with anyone else in class.

On the last day of our workshop, after learning a lot about the Principles of Relationship and after going through a round of Q & As with the participants, she ran up to me just before we ended and told me, "Teacher, I weigh more than a hundred kilograms. I tried many different methods to lose weight and I have spent lots of money to do so (to no avail). Can you help me?"

I gave her an unwavering gaze. When she was asking the question, there seemed a shred of contempt in her eyes. Her nose was upturned, her neck was gently leaning backwards and she was looking at me from the corner of her eyes. It seemed to me a mixture of contempt and disrespect.

Then, I smiled and replied, "A person's weight is very much linked to their psychological state."

"Oh, is that so? Then what should I do?" Wang Juan asked me, her voice full of doubt.

"It seems to me that you do not quite believe what I say. But to me, the weight on your body is not really much of an issue. Quite the contrary,

I think it the state of your mind and the impact that it has on your life that is the real problem."

Wang Juan was still doubtful, "Oh, is that so?"

I teased her and said, "Oh well, anyway, the weight is on your body and not mine. It is up to you how you want to lead your life." I was trying to aggravate her on purpose.

Wang Juan looked at me straight in the eyes and said, "But I am here because I need your help. Other than putting on more and more weight, I am also very unhappy and my relationship with my husband is also very bad."

I looked back straight into her eyes and said, "So do you really want to change?"

"Yes."

I looked at her straight into the eyes one more time and asked her again, "Do you really want to change?"

"Yes," Wang Juan kept her eyes wide opened and nodded her head firmly.

"Even if making this change will mean that you have to pay a price, even if it means you will have to lose something, will you be willing to do that?"

"Yes, I am willing."

"Good, I trust you," and I continued, "I just said that weight is linked to a person's psychological sate, do you know who the person that is linked directly to your weight issue"

"I don't know."

"It's your mother."

The answer seemed to shake her up a little and she stared at me with doubt.

I continued to ask her, "Do you respect your mother?"

Wang Juan thought about it for a while and said, "I love my mother, but she doesn't know how to take care of herself and I always have to take care of her and help her with a lot of things. She does not know what is the best for her."

"So you want to save her, and you want her to lead life according to what you deem as the 'correct' way to lead life?"

"Aren't all children like that?"

"No, not all children are like that. All these children who seem to want to help their parents on the surface are actually unconsciously standing in a higher position than their parents in their own hearts. They think they can save their parents because they know better and do not actually respect their parent's position. When this happens, they will 'become bigger' than their parents and stand in a higher position than their parents in the order of the family system. Do you know what "become bigger" means?"

Wang Juan shook her head.

"When we say 'become bigger' it means that even your body and your weight will become big. If you do not change the attitude you have towards your mother, if you continue not have respect for your mother, you will never be able to reduce your weight and this will affect your body and your mind for the rest of your life."

"But I respect my mother!"

I gave a hearty laugh, "That's ok. Let's take a look and find out."

I asked Wang Juan to choose a workshop participant to represent her mother and I asked her Wang Juan to stand facing her mother about 3 meters away right in the middle of our classroom. Wang Juan saw her mother and wanted to walk forward towards her. But when she took a step forward, her mother took a step backwards. When she took another step forward, her mother took another step backwards.

I asked the lady representing her mother, "What do you feel?"

The representative replied, "I feel that she gives me too much pressure and she seem to be bigger than I am."

I said to Wang Juan, "Look at this, this is how your mother truly feels in her heart. We are now revealing the truth of the matter. You do not respect your mother enough; you are just treating her according to what you think is right and you do not really see what your mother truly needs."

"Then what should I do?"

"I said before that if you want to change, you will have to pay a price. Do you know what is the price you have to pay?"

"I don't know."

"You will need to lose your sense of superiority and arrogance."

"Ok, I am willing to do that."

I said to Wang Juan, "Then please kneel down in front of your mother and move closely towards her."

Wang Juan kneeled down and moved closely towards her mother but her mother started to move backwards. As Wang Juan crawls two steps towards her, she moved two steps backwards.

The mother representative said, "Her heart does not really respect me."

Yes, after all it has been many years that Wang Juan has been unconsciously treating her mother in this way and giving her so much pressure. Should we want her to reaccept Wang Juan, it wouldn't be easy at all.

I turned to Wang Juan and said, "You have to respect your mother from your heart."

Because she was once and again rejected by her mother, Wang Juan started to feel very sad and as she crawled over towards her mother, she started crying and calling out to her. "Mummy... mummy...."

And just like this, Wang Juan started to call out to her mother as she crawled towards her, "Mummy... mummy..."

But her mother kept moving backwards and Wang Juan kept crawling forward.

I let them crawl around in circles in the classroom. They kept moving around the classroom and round after round in the next half an hour.

"Mummy, I am so sorry... Mummy, I am so sorry..."

Wang Juan continued to crawl towards her mother. She started to cry from the bottom of her heart and the sound of her calling out to her mother is starting to sound more and more sincere.

"Mummy, I am so sorry, I was too arrogant. I thought I knew more than you did and I did not respect you." Wang Juan kneeled down on the floor and cried very loudly as she called out to her mother.

Her mother stopped in her tracks. She looked at the crawling and crying Wang Juan but when Wang Juan tried to reach out to touch her, she moved one step backwards again.

Wang Juan started to cry really loudly. She continued to crawl towards her mother and cry out, "Mummy... I am so sorry!" as she continued sobbing.

Another ten minutes or so passed. In the end, Wang Juan kneeled on the floor and gave her mother a few kowtows.

I guided Wang Juan to tell her mother, "Mummy, I am so sorry. I respect that you are my elder and that I am your junior. Please accept me as your daughter again. Please, I beg you."

Wang Juan was all fours on the floor and her hands were outstretched to her mother as if wanting to go closer to her mother. Her mother saw that Wang Juan's attitude has changed considerably and so she stopped moving backwards. Wang Juan extended her hand forward and crawled towards her mother. "Mummy, I am so sorry. I beg you, please accept me."

We saw Wang Juan sprawled on the floor. She moved forward inch by inch and her fingers inched forward slowly towards her mother. In the end, she was finally able to touch her mother's toes.

"Mummy, I beg you... I beg you..."

Wang Juan's cries moved every heart in the room. At this moment, her mother slowly stretched out her hand and touched Wang Juan's head. Wang Juan moved forward and hugged her mother's legs. Her mother finally reaccepted her! They finally returned to the right order between mother and daughter. Her mother is big and Wang Juan is small. At this moment, her mother started crying too. All the sufferings that she had is finally out in the open and acknowledged and because Wang Juan changed her attitude towards the mother, her mother was willing to reaccept her again.

Wang Juan kneeled down in front of her mother and her mother hugged her, Wang Juan hugged tightly back. Everyone in the room was visibly moved. The sight in front of us is one of human kind's most natural order. When a mother gives birth to a child, regardless of what kind of person she is, what she has done, she will always be our mother. She is big and we are small. If our love for our mother goes against this natural order, this will create a disorder in our relationship and will definitely affect both our minds and bodies.

Wang Juan hugged her other tightly and her mother hugged her tightly. At this moment, the love between naturally flowed through them. The mother is finally a mother and the daughter is finally a daughter. We can see a peaceful smile on Wang Juan's face. What can be more beautiful than a child going back to their place and a child going back into the embrace of their mother? Wang Juan's blushing face started to break out into a youthful smile.

After some time Wang Juan finally stood up.

"Very good. You have changed yourself and you have helped yourself."

Wang Juan gave me a deep bow and said, "Thank you, teacher!"

3 months passed and I went to Shenzhen to conduct a workshop. One of Wang Juan's good friend attended my workshop and he said that Wang Juan specially asked him to pass me a message. Wang Juan asked him to tell me that she is currently very healthy mentally and physically. She has already lost more than 30 kilograms and is still continuing to lose weight. Most importantly, she is becoming happier and sexier and the relationship between her and her husband is improving too. They are even planning to have a second kid!

Fat Women Eat Up Their Mothers

Even though Wang Juan loves her mother, but the way she shows her love lacks respect and gives her mother great pressure. Not only was she not aware of the mistake, she even openly declared that her mother should live life according to her rules. When she does that, she is standing in a position that is "bigger" (and more superior) than that of her mother and thus she is going against the Principle of Order. Not only will this sort of love be not helpful for their relationship, it will bring about disorder in their relationship because in this relationship, Wang Juan becomes "big" and her mother becomes "small", thereby manifesting this in her physical size as well. This is the reason why Wang Juan became big (bloated and fat) physically (Hellinger, 2003d).

Until Wang Juan made the awareness and was willing to go back to the position of the child and respect her mother, even though she lost the arrogance that made her want to save her mother, she reclaimed her place in the right order and found back her ease in life. It is therefore only right that she loses all the excess flesh on her body and go back to her own "size". She will also regain her physical and mental health and what makes her even happier is that her relationships with both her mother and husband have improved tremendously.

When a woman does not respect her mother, she will be unable to respect men and this will affect their interpersonal relationships. Because our relationship with our mother is the first interpersonal relationship we have, our relationship with our mother is a reflection of all our relationships with the people around us. Even though Huang Juan was unaware of it, but her attitude towards other people and even her interaction with me during the workshop seemed to carry a slight disrespect. However, when she started to really respect her mother and move back into a suitable position in relation to her mother, her attitude towards the people around also started to change unknowingly. After the constellations, we could tell that she has become more friendly and respectful in her manner towards her peers and towards me. Therefore, when we go back to our positions, not only will our minds go back to the correct size, our bodies will go back to its natural size too. We will move back into the rightful size and order or things in our interpersonal relationships with others.

Principle of Order: Returning To Your Position In The Right Order To Love

What is the "Principle of Order"?

The "Principle of Order" is one of the most important principles in relationships. What it refers to is that everyone in the family system will be given a position based on the order that they are included into the family. Therefore, everyone belongs in their own rightful place in this "sequential order".

For example, when a father and mother get married and form a family, they will become the first in the order of the family system. After that, they give birth to some children and these children will also follow the order that they are born to find their position amongst their siblings. Likewise, in sequential order of time as life is passed down from generation to generation, our ancestors were here in the family before us and so they are bigger than us as they were here before us; our children, grandchildren came into the family later than we did and so they are smaller than us as they came into the family after we did. This sort of sequential order is a natural development. In our Chinese tradition, we always emphasize on "having respect based on the order of seniority" (長幼有序) in our families. By the grace of our human nature and by the grace of nature, a family will only be natural and harmonious when they follow the Principle of Order.

If a person is disrespectful to their parents, this means that they have already gone against the Principle or Order. However, it is very difficult to be aware when people go against this Principle unconsciously. Most of the time, these people think that their actions are justifiable because they think they are doing it out of love. What they are not aware is that their love is running on the wrong path and is a form of disorderly love. They will unconsciously start to stand in a taller position when they interact with their parents and will think that only this sort of love is the right sort of love. When this happens, the very strict Principle of Order will teach us a lesson. This sort of arrogance and superiority will cause our life to be unhappy and unsuccessful. In serious cases, it may even result in sickness and death. Regrettably, most people are only aware of this when they have paid a high price for it. Only then do they learn to go back to their own position in the order to love (Hellinger et al., 1998).

Let's imagine how it would be for us if our children do not respect us and want to interfere with our lives, with some of them going to the extent of trying to take over our pain by making their lives miserable. As a parent, how would you feel if this happens? We would definitely be unhappy, don't you agree? That is because this sort of arrogance goes against the order within us. At the same time, if our children do not live the life we have given them to the fullest, because of their blind love and desire to help us, it would be something that all parents find intolerable. By the same reasoning, if we treat our parents in the same way, this is how they would feel too.

"Respecting your parent's destiny" does not mean that we do not or cannot help our parents. Quite the contrary, it is because we love them, we therefore have to learn to love them in a more mature way instead of practicing blind love which often ends up in failure. The most important thing is this: when we love our parents and would like to help them, we have to hold a respectful attitude towards them. We should love our parents from the position of a child and not stand in a position that is "taller" or "bigger" than our parents to try to save them.

Someone once asked me. "What if our parents are really at fault? Then what should we do?" The Chinese traditional classics, Di Zi Gui (弟子規/ Student's Rules) says, "When the parents make a mistake, counsel them to make a change. When counseling them, make sure your expression is pleasant and your voice, soft. If the counseling is not accepted, wait until parents are in a good mood and counsel them again. Should they still not listen, weeping and wailing should follow, and beatings are to be borne without complaint." This means to say that when our parents make a mistake, we should gently and carefully counsel them. We have to be sincere and our tone, pleasant and soft. When our parents do not listen to our counsel, we should wait for a suitable time and place when they are in a good mood and continue to counsel them. Even if we have to cry our hearts out, we have to beg our parents to change for the better. And even if they were to scold us or beat us up, we have to continue to counsel them nicely. From start to end, the foundation of the whole process is that it must be conducted in a respectful manner towards our parents.

Therefore, just having love is not enough. In addition, we need to learn **how to learn**. If we want to become more successful and have a smoother life, enjoy a more harmonious relationship in the family and have better relationships with our parents, we have to follow the Principle of Order and return to our position to love them. This sort of orderly love is a love that follows the principles of life and nature and is the type of love we have to learn.

Inner Constellation Exercise: Reconciliation With Your Mother

This Inner Constellation might seem very difficult for some people at the start. However, I urge you to please give it a good try and try to follow it slowly. Our mothers may not be perfect and if we have too many expectations on her or wishes for her to be someone she is not, we will be unable to see the truth of life. It is only through this mother did we get our lives. If we had a different mother, we would be totally different and wouldn't be ourselves. Therefore, it is important to accept the truth of life and find reconciliation with our mother as this is in actual fact, a reconciliation with our self. When we can return to our position of love, we would be able to feel easy and freedom and be able to shine in our lives.

However, should you have an issue with your father; you may also use this exercise to find reconciliation with your father. All you need to do is to change the words "mother" to "father".

Now gather ourselves together
Go back to our centers
Imagine our mother is standing right in front of us
Connect with our mother
Look at her face
Look at her eyes
From the bottom of your heart, tell her…

"Dear mother
You brought me to this world
This is a fact
However, I neglected this truth
I may have blamed you and complained about what you have done
I may have thought that you were not good enough and tried to change you
But now
I am willing to reaccept this truth
Life is passed on from you to my body
And only through this special person like you
Can I receive this life

*Can I become the person I am now
If I were born into another family
I wouldn't be me anymore
I would become someone else*

*Because of you
I am here
Regardless of what happened between us
We will be unable to deny this important fact
This is the most important for me
Only you can give me this life
Everything you have given me is precious
Should I require other things
I can find them elsewhere
But only you can give me such a precious gift
Thank you
Thank you
You are my right mother
Other than you
I don't want anyone else"*

*After that
Use your own way to show gratitude to your mother and thank her
You can give a bow or kowtow to her or you can give her a big hug*

*After that
Slowly take a step backwards
Return to your own position
Take a deep breath
And return to the present*

Mum, I Love You And I Love Dad Too (Facing The Conflict Between Your Parents)

Hellinger (2001a) emphasized that after we get married, our current family takes precedence over our original family. But this does not mean we are cut off from our original family but it is more of "I will now take good care of my own family, should you need me, I will do the right thing." This should be the correct order in the onward legacy of life.

People who commit crimes or acts of domestic violence will be punished by the Principle. But other than paying a price for their actions, are they trying to say something with their actions? Is there a deeper reason for their behavior? Other than legally making them responsible for their actions and punishing them, if we are able to find out the deeper motivations behind these behaviors, we will be able to help them and keep them from repeating their mistakes.

I have been invited to the Taiwanese Public Prosecutor's office to give lessons to some people who were on probation. These people have mostly been involved in crimes of violence like injuring other people, domestic violence, arson, etc. There were about umpteen of us and we formed a circle for our session. Because they were not there voluntarily, when we first started our workshop, they were passive and some of them were also having a huge resistance to the workshop.

Guo Long is one of them and he is a tall and handsome young man. He used to be policeman and the reason he was on probation was because his wife got into a fight with his mother and in a moment of anger, he hit his wife to protect his mother. Because he practices martial arts, his wife was very badly injured. Other than being put on probation, the court also did not allow to go near his wife and his children.

"Do you regret it?" I asked him.

"Yes I do. But I don't know what came over me at that moment, it was as if I was totally unable to control my emotions, especially when I

saw my wife quarreling with my mum, I felt as if I was being swallowed up by the anger. Now I regret it very much but my wife is unwilling to forgive me... I wish I can see my children again."

"Would you like to control yourself so that the same thing will not happen again?"

"Or course I do! But I can't stand it whenever my wife gets into a fight with my mum. Whenever I see them doing that, I would lose control and my anger will erupt like volcano. That is why I hit her."

"Good, then let's explore what is hiding behind these emotions and see if there is any way to improve the situation."

I decided to use family constellations to explore and thus invited four people to represent Guo Long himself, his wife, his mother and his father.

"Now I want you to calm down. Please arrange these people accordingly to how the relationship between the four of you look like in your heart. Take into consideration the distance between them and also the direction they might be facing."

Without any interference from anyone, Guo Long focused intently on placing them in the correct position in the classroom.

The moment he was done, we could see the subconscious dynamics in his family very clearly. He placed himself between his father and his mother, his back was facing his mother and his face was facing his father. He opened his arms and looked like he was protecting his mother and trying to fight his dad. But he placed his wife very far away from these three people.

"Did you know?" I asked him, "Systemic Constellations can show the subconscious dynamics within your family. Here, we can see clearly who is the person you really wanted to protect and who is the person you really wanted to fight."

Guo Long was shocked by the image he saw in front of him. He had never thought he would be stuck between his father and mother and would fight against his father. Looking at this image, he started to recall some childhood incidents involving his parents. "Since young, my mother and father have often been quarreling with each other. Once, I even saw my father hit my mother and my mother would confide in me whenever she was in anguish."

"Yes, you love your mother very much and want to protect her, that is why you unconsciously took on the anger she felt towards you father. But because you also love your father and because he is your elder, you did not have an outlet to vent this anger."

"Yes, even when they quarrel now, my heart gets tangled up in a mess and I very often get very affected by it."

"That is right, you have accumulated a lot of anger in your heart and it is like a volcano. That is why when your wife quarreled with your mother, you are unable to control and would unleash all the past anger you felt towards your father on your wife."

Guo Long nodded his head furiously. "I finally understand! Usually, I have a very good relationship with my wife but once she starts to talk bad about my mother, I just cannot contain my anger."

"Yes, and that is because you are in the wrong position, in the wrong order. You are standing in the same position as your father and mother, hoping to change the relationship between the two of them."

"So that is what it is. Then, what should I do?"

"It is very easy but yet at the same time very difficult. You have to consciously go back to the position that belongs to you."

"How should I do that?"

"Are you ready?"

Guo Long replied with vigour, "Yes, I am ready!"

I invited Guo Long's representative to go back to his seat and got Guo Long to represent himself. After that, I asked him to make a conscious decision and very slowly walk out of the position between his parents. Then I asked him to take a step backwards and face his parents.

Guo Long was very focused. He slowly walked out and turned around to face his parents.

Following that, I guided Guo Long to say to his parents, "Mother, since young, I have been watching the two of your quarrel, I was really upset and I really hope the two of you can get along better with each other."

Tears started to well up in Guo Long's eyes and he started to choke as he started to repeat the sentence.

"But I am only your son, I am really unable to help when you get into a fight. Mother, I am so sorry I am unable to help you…"

Tears start to glide down his face as he said that.

"Mother, I love you and I really would like to share the burden with you, but I love father too."

"Please forgive me if I choose to go near to father."

Guo Long's mother started to tear as well. Her body started to sway and she looked at her son sadly.

I guided Guo Long to continue, "Dear Mother, now I will return the anger belonging to you back to you."

His mother continued to cry sadly she gently put her hands on Guo Long's shoulders to support him. Looking at how much suffering her child is experiencing, she was deeply affected by what she saw and it seemed as if she was finally able to accept it.

Following that, Guo Long turned to face his Father. All of a sudden, he kneeled down facing his father on his own accord.

He continued to cry and as he cried, he continued to repent, "Father, I am sorry. I have never really respected you as my father in my heart. I thought you were not good enough to mother and the fact of the matter is that I looked down on you."

Guo Long hugged his father's legs tightly and continued to cry as he repented.

"I am sorry; I know I am at fault. Can you please accept me as your son again?"

His father also started to tear. And it is only natural that he feels sad. All this while, all the effort he has made for his son has never been truly acknowledged. And how would he be not aware of the hatred his son has towards him? However, the great father continued to contribute silently to the growth of his children and continued to nurture them till adulthood, never once ceasing to support this family.

With his steadfast love, Guo Long's father gave Guo Long a pat on his shoulder and helped him up. Father and son hugged in a manly embrace and yet revealing a certain tenderness between them.

After a while, I said to Guo Long, "There is something very important that you have to say to your father and mother: Dear Father and Mother, I respect the way you interact with each other and now, I want to go back to my position as a son."

Guo Long made a deep bow to his parents and very sincerely repeated, "Dear Father and Mother, I respect the way you interact with each other and now, I want to go back to my position as a son."

At this moment, something miraculous happened. When Guo Long made a deep bow and said those words, his parents were actually willing to turn and face each other—without Guo Long blocking in between, they are now able to come to face with the relationship between them.

I pointed out this image to Guo Long.

"Yes, I understand now!" Guo Long seemed suddenly enlightened.

When everything goes back to its correct order, Guo Long was finally able to turn around and look at his wife.

He took a step towards his wife.

"I am sorry," Guo Long lowered his head. "I loved my mother too much and I did not really take a good look at you."

"I am sorry."

Guo Long sincerely apologized to his wife and slowly he moved closer and held her hands.

"Now, I am back!"

The representative who represented his wife felt his sincerity and told him that she still loves him.

"Please give me another chance."

The representative representing his wife nodded her head, her eyes were filled with tears.

They embraced in a silent hug for a while and at this point, I ended the constellations.

A month later, I was still giving lessons at the same place because these people were to be continuing their workshop for two consecutive months. When I met Guo Long again, I asked him how he was and he said his father and mother were quarrelling again.

He added, "But Teacher, last time I would jump out to stop them. Because I attended your workshop, I know I should go back to my position. The miraculous thing is that I no longer feel that sort of anger anymore. Also, because I know they love to listen to the oldies, I bought two Cai Qin (a famous Taiwanese singer who sings many Chinese oldies) concert tickets for them. Even though they had some sort of quarrel, they felt that since their son already bought them tickets, they had to go to the concert no matter what. In the end, the held hands and left to watch the concert together."

"That's excellent!"

"What is even more amazing is that my wife is willing to pick up my calls now. After I apologized to her, she is now willing to let my son talk to me over the phone. She said she will think about shortening the separation period. I am really, really happy! Thank you so much, Teacher Chou!

Every single one of us were so happy to share Guo Long's happy news. I was also very happy to see that the students in the class who used to be passive, reserved and resistant are starting to become more engaged in class. At the start, the probation officer had to monitor them to make sure that they would attend the workshops but as our workshop continued, everyone automatically turned up without prompting. At the same time, everyone in the class was given a chance to explore the psychological reason and family dynamics that has resulted in their actions. Some of them even came over to ask me questions after class, enquiring about how to improve the situation in their family. Some of them shared with me that they have gained out of the workshop…

Yes, when people are once again seen and accepted, everyone would want their life to become even better!

Transformation of Family Violence

As a police officer, Guo Long was well aware that beating his wife is a criminal offence. Yet, at that very moment, he was controlled by a huge anger and seemed to totally lose himself. Given that this was not a one off incident, just punishing him and counseling him is not enough as this anger is not only his to begin with. If we did not find out the psychology behind this domestic violence, this sort of incident will certainly happen again and again. During such situations, Systemic Constellations would be a good tool to explore the deeper psychology dynamics of a person and their family and also a good way to find the key to a solution.

Through Systemic Constellations, we discovered the hidden dynamics behind Guo Long's violence towards his wife was that he had wanted to protect his mother and fight against his father. He has transferred the anger he had for his father onto his wife. Eventually, the quarrel between his mother and wife became like an ignited fuse and caused him to hit his wife. Guo Long started to wake up from his blind love and started to understand the root of his anger towards his wife. He also learnt to move back into his position of a son and respect the way his parents interact with each other and only when this happens, without Guo Long stuck in between them, his parents are able to really face up to their relationship issues. Finally, Guo Long learnt how to release himself from the entanglements of his original family to take good care of his own family.

Going Against The Principle Of Order: The Reason Men Desire Incest

Let us analyze this example on a deeper level. Research in psychology often talks about a type of "incest" (called Oedipus Complex). It does not refer to a physical form of incest but a psychological one. It states that both sons and daughters have got a sub conscious secret buried in their hearts-- they all feel that they are better partners for their fathers or mothers (Hellinger, 2001b).

When the son gets embroiled in his parent's relationship, a triangular relationship is formed. If a son is too close to his mother, he will become his mother's emotional extramarital affair. The mother will then unconsciously lead her son to stand in the place of his father. And once the son gets married and has his own wife, the issue will become even more obvious. That's because another triangular relationship is now formed. The wife of the son will be unable to stand in her position as her position has already been taken up by her mother-in-law.

This sort of confusion between the position of a husband and son will result in a fight between the wife and mother-in-law for the position to be partner of the son and it is often the deeper psychological dynamic responsible for fights between the daughters-in-law and mothers-in-law.

If the earlier generation does not resolve this issue, the future generation will start to repeat this pattern. The son will notice that the father cares more for his mother and therefore tend to care more for his own mother and thus gets closer to his mother. When he gets married in future, this pattern will continue on to the next generation (Fang & Shih, 2000).

This sort of psychological incest (Oedipus Complex) goes against The Principle of Order. So how do we untangle this chain of entanglements? The answer is that the son has to resist the temptation to step into his parent's relationship. That means he has to say to his mother, "Dear mother, I am only your son. I am unable to take care of you in place of father. I love you but I love father too, now, I would like to return to my position as a son. The same logic applies to daughters.

On the other hand, this also a good reminder that as parents, we should take up the courage to face up to our relationship issues and we should be aware and alert to the fact that we should not unconsciously drag our children into out relationship.

Inner Constellation: Tribute To Life

When we receive the gift of "life", it is so precious that it is virtually impossible to repay our parents for it. However, should we be able to express our gratitude towards our parents in our hearts, we will be able to able to have the experience being in the flow of life and feel a sense of wholeness and peace. It will also allow us to go back into our path of life and we will know and understand what is it we have to do next.

From another point of view, this tribute it is a best way to reorganize ourselves. It is a constellations process involving our parents that we conduct in our hearts and it is especially useful when our parents are in a fight, in disharmony or even in the midst of a divorce. It can also help us pull through these unhappy past events and allow us to move back into our correct positions. When we go through this process in our minds, our world on the outside will start to change too.

I invite everyone to move back to your own positions
Consolidate yourselves together
Return to your centre
Now imagine your biological parents standing in front of you
Look at them
If you have never seen them before
You can still imagine two people standing in front of you
Because the fact is they do exist or have existed before
Now
Please look at our biological parents
And say to them

Dear father
Dear mother
Thank your for passing life on to me
In order to give me this life
We have all paid a price
From other people
I am unable to receive this life
Only you can give me this life
Because you give, I accept
You are big, I am small
In my heart
You are the right father and mother for me
No one else can replace you

Dear father and mother
You will always be my father and mother

This relationship will never change
Even if you are separated
Even if there are any changes taking place between the two of you
I respect the decision the both of you made
I respect the way you interact with each other
But in my body
You are always joined in oneness
And will never be separated
Because my life
Is the best evidence of the joining of your love

Dear father and mother
I respect the way you face your problems
Now, I will return to my position as a child
And return to the position belonging to me
To experience my life
I will use the life you gave me
To do some really good things
Letting this life be brilliant
This is the way I will repay you

If possible
I will be like you
I will pass on this life to my children
Just like what you have done for me
If I do not have my own children
I will still make good use of this life
So that the love you have given me
Can be passed on to more people who need it

After that, take a deep bow in front of your parents
The deeper the better
The slower the better
It would be best if you can kneel down
And give a kowtow
Make three resounding kowtows
This is the highest form of respect and gratitude we can give our parents
It is also the highest form of humility and respect

We can show to the great source of life behind our parents

Chapter 4: Parent And Child Relationships

A child's cognitive development is no different from the process of learning through social interaction. Therefore, improving the child's current relationship will be very helpful to the child's cognitive development.

-- Lev S. Vygotsky

Children:
The Mirror Of The Family

Lin (2015) observed that children are like the mirror of a family. They will reflect the actual situation in the family and they are the most direct reflection of what the parents are teaching as "role models". Because a child will imitate his parent's actions and interactions, in this case, "action speaks louder than words". Therefore, a parent's actions by example are more important than what they tell the child. I feel that 'modelling after other people' through the superficial information they receive via observation is one of the ways that children could learn basic behaviours. However, it is the parent's deeper psychological state that will affect the state of a child's deeper psychology. But the deeper psychological state of parents is often hidden and unseen, so just how do children pick them up? The deeper psychological state of a child is actually a reflection of the subconscious information that they received. And this subconscious information is like what Martin Bubor says, "The subconscious information exists between individuals," and it exists within the relationships they have with each other. Therefore, this means that what our child is really learning and reacting to is not our superficial actions or words but the deeper "relationship" information that we have passed on to them (Roy, 2016).

Based on my observation, amongst all the information that children learn and react to, the one that influences them most is the **relationship between their parents** and the **power of their family system**. But not every relative is included in our family system, only a special group of people belong to our system. I will explain this in detail later in this chapter.

The relationship between the parents will not only include their relationship as husband and wife but also their relationship with their children. Even though different children react differently to the same issues, but based on the many family cases that I have done, this is what I have observed:

1. If the children start to act lost, for example, they lose an interest in learning, have unstable emotions, show conflicting emotions, what he or she could possibly be reflecting is some sort of imbalance or lack of clarity in the husband-and-wife relationship between the parents.

2. If the child starts to lose concentration, becomes dependent or is prone to mixing with the wrong crowd, what he or she is usually reflecting is some sort of double standards practiced by the parents, some split in the husband-and-wife relationship or a lack of a sense of belonging towards the family.

3. When the mother is often absent, the child will tend to feel empty and depressed easily. They will be filled with anxiety and panic and tend to be indecisive. They will also tend to have more inter-relationship problems and find it hard to express themselves or to join or connect with other people.

4. If the father is absent, sons will tend to become addicted to something. For example, they might become addicted to computer games, smoking, drinking or drugs. Daughters will tend to mature too early and may suffer from overeating. They will also become interested in mature men and long for someone to protect them.

5. When one of the parents have a desire to leave the family or die, the child will subconsciously receive the information and may try to run away from home, become chronically ill, meet with danger or meet with accidents in response to it. In extreme cases, they might even end up dead. That is because the fantasy in the little minds of theirs is "If I take your place and leave this family, we will never need to be separated from each other."

In addition to this, other than the influence from the relationship between their parents, another huge influence that will affect a child immensely is the influence coming from "the power of their family systems". Often, this is even more difficult to observe, especially if it involves any unfinished business that the previous generations might have had. But just like a mirror, the child will reflect whatever is going on within the family. Sometimes, the influence from the family system may overpower the influence from a child's parents and cause the child to exhibit inexplicable emotions and baffling behavioural symptoms. For example, children will secretly repeat the destiny, suffering and symptoms of those who have been excluded by other family members. The good news is, through the method of Systemic Constellations, we are able to better understand the dynamics behind our family systems. Thus, we will be able to understand the causes of such emotions and behaviour exhibited by the child. We can also understand how we can change for the better and understand what are the principles binding the relationship between parent and child. Therefore, should you want to understand the deeper psychology behind a child and find out how they will turn out when they grow up, all you need to do is to understand the relationship between their parents and the dynamics behind their family system (Mahr, 1998).

How Systemic Constellations Can Help Our Children

First. I would like to briefly explain how I apply Systemic Constellations on helping the children.

One of the characteristics of Systemic Constellations is that the process does not require the attendance of the whole family. Therefore, the way I usually facilitate cases would be to either only include the parents in the workshop or even more ideally, to get the parents to attend the workshop together with their young children or teenagers. Then, they can come together to do something for the child who may have psychological or behavioural issues. Through the processes and learning that takes place in the workshop, they will be able to improve the situation in the whole family. Whenever necessary, I will also do the individual constellations with the child through the use of props such as puppets and coloured paper.

Issues related to the growth and development of a child is a focal point I care deeply about. I have been invited many times by the court to conduct Systemic Constellations workshops for delinquents under their charge. Many of these delinquents engage in stealing, vandalism, drug abuse or prostitution. Usually some twenty, thirty young people will come together for a workshop. Some of then are accompanied by their parents and some of them are accompanied by their guardians or even their probation officers. This is a great practice as both parents and child will be able to understand how the children are affected by their family systems and the parents can no longer only focusing on blaming the children. At the same time, it also allows the parents to see the effect that the family system has on their children and allows them to understand what are the needed adjustments they should make in future and what their common goal is. Those who provide help for the child and the probation officers will also be able understand the family and child better and know which direction they can focus on to provide maximum help to the child (Hellinger, 2001a).

Every year, I will take some time out and conduct charity workshops for public welfare units to counsel children who are disabled or children from disadvantaged families. I will also provide counseling to high-risk group students which include students suffering from depression, dejection, suicidal thoughts and self-inflicted injuries. During our workshops, we learn from each other and are able to see how we are affected by our families. Through the workshops, we can see how our children's love is causing them pain. We can also see how children start to change as a result of Systemic Constellations and how afterward, with the help of their teachers and counselors, they are then able to find the strength to face up to their life's challenges. I really hope that all the children and parents who truly need help will take my advice and attend at least one systemic constellations workshop. The workshop will allow your children and allow you to create a better future.

Another point worth mentioning is this just how old does a child have to be to attend a Systemic Constellations workshop? In my workshops, the youngest participant I have had was 3 years old. He attended together with his father and mother. Do you think the child does not understand? That is where you are wrong. In my workshops, I have observed that children are often more sensitive and their reactions and experiences often sharper and more direct because they are so pure within. Therefore the impact the family's order and system has on them is much bigger. If there is a problem with the child, it is important for the parents to remember that the key to solving the issue would lie in their learning and their change. If the parent is willing to change and if this family system has a positive change, the child will also change positively and have a brighter future filled with even more hope.

Symptoms Of Your Children's Behaviour- Helping Children Face Up To Divorce

Husbands and wives may one day become separated. However, parent and child relationships are forever; even if we are no longer able stay as a couple, we should still help each other become a pair of excellent parents (Mahr, 1998).

Five years ago, because of her husband's extramarital affair, Liu Fang was in deep anguish. Even though they have since gotten a divorce and gone on their separate ways, the hate and anger that she felt stayed on in her heart and she was unable to get rid of it.

But because of her children, Liu Fang has decided that she will face up to this issue now.

"My daughter is doing her 5th year in her primary school. The doctor says that she is unable to concentrate well and I am very worried. Even her teacher will make fun of her in front of the other students and I am afraid she will be traumatized by this." Liu Fang tried to explain her concerns about her daughter.

"When a person is unable to concentrate or focus, they will tend to turn their heads and look this way and that way. If the father and mother are not on good terms or are divorced, the child will tend to look at her father and then turn her head to look at her mother. One can imagine it is only natural that they would be unable to focus on any one point." I said.

When I invited Liu Fang to set up the constellations for her, her daughter and her ex-husband, it was just as it is in her current situation. In order to balance her need for both mother's love and father's love, her daughter was facing both separated parents and had to keep changing her focus, looking at her father for a while and turning to look at her mother for a while.

What about Liu Fang herself? She was standing right in the middle with her back to her ex-husband.

"It has been five years, that's enough," I said.

For the sake of her daughter and for the sake of her own self, Liu Fang considered making a choice and choosing the possibility of reconciliation. But the moment she thought of the betrayal she experienced; her face started to show anger. It was as if the wound in her heart was still throbbing with pain!

"Reconciliation does not mean that you agree to what he has done to you. It is more of a 'I am so angry with what you have done and I am still unable to forgive you but I agree that you are still the father of my daughter.'"

Liu Fang listened to my words very intently. At the same time, she kept gasping for breath. It was as if other than being angry, she was also trying to find the strength to break through the current situation.

At this moment, the child inside the constellations looked at her mother and started to look very frightened. Liu Fang's ex-husband continued to lower his head and did not dare to look at her at all.

"This is indeed a very tough and difficult process for you."

"Unless he apologizes to me!"

Liu Fang shouted angrily at her husband, "I am so angry with you!"

She continued again, "I am so angry with you!"

With her fist clenched and her jaws clenched even tighter, she turned around and turned her back towards her ex-husband.

I continued to encourage her, "Yes, you are indeed unable to forgive him. But your child is innocent, for the sake of your child, the both of you have to give it a try."

Liu Fang finally managed to turn herself around to face her husband. Her child's mood and feelings were also undergoing a massive change as she turned around. After all, blood is thicker than water, a child is usually the driving force for the growth of their parents.

Liu Fang steadied herself and told her daughter, "The separation between your dad and I was not what I wanted. Your dad did something to me and I am still unable to forgive him. But this has got nothing to do with you. You will forever be the crystallization of the love between myself and your father."

Listening to her mother's words, the child started to cry. Looking at her tearing child, Liu Fang gently said to her, "I love you and you can love your father. Even though we are divorced, he will forever be your father."

A miraculous change took place after that. After hearing to what her mother said, her child started to calm down. Indeed, only when we face up to our issues can we resolve them.

Just like how Liu Fang admitted that the child's father will always be her father, Liu Fang seemed to understand that no matter how much anger she feels, it does not change the facts at all. The only way she can complete and create a wholeness inside the heart of her child is to move beyond their husband-and-wife relationship and move into the parent and child relationship they have with their child.

Liu Fang told her daughter, "If you want to visit your father, I will agree to it."

Once Liu Fang said that to her, the child turned and look at her father with a slight tinge of fear but there was a big smile on her face.

Next, I guided Liu Fang to say some important words that should be said between a couple when they decide to part. I asked her to say them slowly and told her that it is important that these words come from the heart. "Thank you for treating me well in the past. I will treasure that in my heart. All the good I have done for you; I have done it happily. If you are willing, you can treasure them in your heart.

Towards what happened between us, you were at fault and I was also at fault. With regards to the things, I have done wrong, I take up my responsibility for it. As for those that you have done wrongly, I will leave your part of the responsibility to you.

Thank you for being my husband, you will forever have a place in my heart.

Thank you for accompanying me through this journey in life. You have enriched my life I bless that you will also find your own happiness."

As she started to weep, Liu Fang was finally able to say these words out.

The child gave us feedback of how she felt, 'I feel as I am much more comfortable now. Now I feel I don't have to think too much or get too worried. I can finally calm myself down and focus."

I asked Liu Fang, "Did you hear that? The child can settle down and focus."

Liu Fang took a deep breath. Her heart seemed to feel more at ease.

"For the sake of the children, even if a couple were to be separated, they have to work hard on helping the other party become a good father or mother. Only in this way will the child feel a sense of completeness in their hearts."

Liu Fang nodded her head. Instead of looking back at the past in anger, she now looks forward to her future with a smile on her face.

The Principle Of Wholeness: Divorced Couple, United As Parents

In the past few years, the rate of divorce all over the world has been rising rapidly. On the average, out of every 3-4 couples, one will end up in a divorce. Therefore, the act of "divorce" has become one of the most important impacts a parent can have on a child. It is impossible for a couple to be together forever. Even if they are very much in love, there will also come a day where they will have to part in death. Even though we cannot avoid the physical separation, spiritually though, once a couple has lived together for a certain period of time, should they have to part for one reason or another, they will have to find a good way to handle it and not just flippantly break up or they will most certainly affect their children (Mahr, 1998).

From the many examples I have observed, even though some couples may have been divorced but because the knot in their hearts have not been undone, this dynamic will still continue to affect their children. So what happens in the deep recesses of these children's hearts? Deep in their hearts, there is a hidden voice which says; "It is all my fault. I have to be responsible for the separation of my father and mother." And so, these children will start to behave strangely or have strange incidents happening to them. For example, they might often go into conflict with their parents, they might become emotionally unstable, unable to stay focused, lose interest in learning, fight with their classmates, act dangerously or perhaps even allowing themselves to contract strange diseases. The ultimate aim of having all that happen to help their parents be on good terms again and to compensate for the separation of their parents.

Therefore, if the relationship issues between the couple are not resolved, there will be little we can do for the child if we were to merely correct their behaviours or situation. Even if we were to do our best to help the child, there is a limit to the amount of improvement we can see. As long as the source of the hidden dynamics remains unresolved, the power of the entanglement will still continue to pull the child in. To the child, this dynamic is the most important thing in his or her life and such is a child's love for their parents that they will even go to the extent of sacrificing for their parents.

Hellinger (2001a) has a very important insight: Because the power behind this dynamic is very strong, it makes us blind. Thus, it is very difficult for the child to walk out of it on their own. Therefore, parents have to help their children and the key to that would be for the parents become united as one. This doesn't mean that the couple has to be together again but it is important to let the child feel that "**even if the affinity between both parents have come to an end, the parent and child bond and relationship will always continue on.**" So the parents have to help the child as one body and allow the child to have the experience that his or her parents are still ONE. If possible, please allow the child to interact with the other party and help the other party become a good parent. Even if the other party is not there physically, we have to show in our hearts, through our attitudes, that we still respect their father/mother. For example, if the child were to do well while playing ball with his friends, the mother might say, "If your father were here, he would be very happy." Or if the child gets very good results in school, the father could say, "If your mother could see this, she would feel so proud of you." Through such actions, even though the other parent is not present, the child would feel as if they do exist in their world and feel as if that parent is also accompanying them while they are growing up.

But do take note that children are very sensitive. If you were to just pay lip service and think otherwise deep in your heart, they would feel that you are consciously or even unconsciously denying their mother/father's position and identity in their life; besides, every child has the right to know their father/mother. But very often, because of their conflict or separation with their other half, parents tend to negate or deny their other halves. Sometimes, they might talk about their other half in a belittling way or they might even be reluctant to let their children meet the other parent. All these are ways of depriving our children of their basic human rights and it very much goes against the Principle of Wholeness. The child will definitely feel this separation (Hellinger et al., 1998).

Therefore, the parents have to first be united as one in their hearts. Given time, a child will slowly learn to really trust them and when that happens, the child will naturally feel a sense of wholeness in their heart.

A Mum's Second Pain- Adolescent Children

When children move into their teenage years, the role of education will fall heavily on the father. Because this is the time where the child will learn how to become an adult and not rely on their mother for protection. To the mother, this is as good as having labour pains the all over again (Lin, 2014).

Every year, the Taiwan Family Support Community Fund will invite me to hold workshops for some charity organizations working with the disadvantaged. One year, my workshop participants were a group people belonging to high-risk families.

Mei Ru was holding on to a crutch. At 45 years old, this petite lady hobbled to my side. After she settled down on her seat, I slowly turned to look at her for a while and then I started to talk to her.

"What happened to your leg?"

With a somewhat fake smile, Mei Ru said, "Originally, it was nothing. Later, it started to curve and slowly shrink."

"How long has it been in like that?"

Mei Ru did not reply me and stared blankly in front of her, lost in her own world. Following that, she suddenly felt a surge of emotion and even though she tried to use her hand to cover her mouth and her nose and tried very hard to suppress the emotion, she eventually lost control and started sobbing, her red eyes started to fill with tears.

"If we keep holding on to the past..." I said softly.

Mei Ru took a deep breath and forcefully said, "Sometimes I am so angry, the stress is immense and I feel like hitting someone and sometimes I feel like I want to die. I really feel that I can't take it anymore!"

"So, what is the past that you are holding on to? What is it that you are holding on to in your heart?" I asked her again.

Mei Ru looked elsewhere, not willing to answer directly. Unsure of herself, she continued, "Is it because my husband used our house as a mortgage to the loansharks that I have no place to live in now?"

"Whether that is the reason for that, only you will know best. How old are your children?"

"One is 18, one is 19... Erm... or is it 20?" Mei Ru started to fumble and seemed confused.

She couldn't remember how old her children were. It is obvious that her life has been seriously stagnant and we don't know how long it has been since her life came to a standstill.

"You are not looking at the present, you are living in the past and you did not move forward."

Mei Ru showed a bitter expression and thought about all the past 10 years of her bitter life. She thought she had finally met her true love but he turned out to be a heartbreaker who caused her to lose her happiness. It was not easy but she finally brought up her children but her children did not want to go to school and caused her even more worry and sadness. To add to that, she had a bad fall two years ago, this resulted in her leg shrinking terribly.

She heaved a loud sigh and finally shared her story. But being able to talk about and give an honest description of the past did not help her feel any better. Instead, she revisited all the anger that she felt through the years.

"It has been 10 years. Your husband's mistake has given you nothing but pain. Perhaps 10 years does not seem like a long time. But in a blinking of an eye, another 10 years will have gone by. Is there anything you hope that you can change for yourself?"

"My second son is very rebellious. If I asked him something, he will retort me in many words. He plays truant and doesn't study..." Mei Ru was filled with emotion as she described the situation with her second son.

I put Meiru, her children and her ex-husband into a constellations. Through the process of Systemic Constellations, we exposed a fact that gave Mei Ru a big shock: the child's situation seems to be similar to that of his father.

"Now you can see the needs in the deep recess of your child's heart. Every child will need to connect with their father. The more you deny the child's father, the more the child will want to be like his father."

Mei Ru started panting forcefully, she was somewhat anxious and definitely angry. She started to think back about her past. Back then, out of her consideration for her husband, she decided to go out and work. Unfortunately, her husband became obsessed with gambling and it eventually caused the family to break up in tragedy. In the past 10 years, Mei Ru and her children have not uttered the word, "father" even though the children still long for their father and even though Mei Ru still has many unreleased emotions and feelings towards him.

"They never mentioned their father and I never once mentioned him as well. I don't know what they are thinking but I just want them to be independent but my second son would often disappear without even informing me. He thinks that I favour my eldest son. When I was working, he spent a lot of time with his father. There is a great distance between us, I don't even know..."

"Mei Ru, I have seen many families in this situation. If the parents are divorced and are not reconciled, the eldest child will want to help the mother and the second child becomes like his father and leave their home."

Mei Ru started to focus on what is happening inside the constellations.

Indeed, just as the representatives have shown, even though her son kept a distance from his father, he was following the footsteps of his father and moving together with his eye on his father's back view.

"A father has his own life experiences. He borrows money, gambles and loses it all. All these are his life experiences. He will not want his son to repeat his life experience. Your son needs his father to pass him his life experiences. The more you want to keep him by your side to protect him, the more a boy his age will want to rebel and push this mother away. If you were to continue to be good to him, he will be unable to move into the next stage of his growth. Currently, the person he needs most is his father."

Mei Ru breathed out for a long, long time. She was finally willing to say to her ex-husband, "Your son needs you. He is already 19 years old. He needs your experience so that he can see his path."

The moment she finished saying that, her son stopped following the father around and started to look down on the floor. Her ex-husband also turned around to look at Mei Ru and their son.

Mei Ru started to cry, "Please help our son. This is the best I can do."

"Yes, this is all that a mother can do. At this point, you will have to hand it over to his father or to his school. If the mother can understand that her child will also need to be connected with his father, she will know how to help him."

"But I don't know where his father is now?"

"That is why you need to practice and learn to use another way to allow father and son to connect even if your ex is not physically with your son. Yesterday, didn't I teach everyone how to do it? We have to praise the child about his strong points which are similar to his dad?"

"His strong points which are similar to his dad?" Mei Ru nodded her head and smiled.

"Yes, what sort of virtues does your son's father have?"

"Mmm.. he has good interpersonal relationships; he has a lot of friends."

"So how will you say it to your child? Let's practice now."

"Zhi Yu, you are like your father, you have good interpersonal skills."

"That's very good Mei Ru but you have to be more sincere. This has to come from the heart. Let's practice some more. Your son will be very happy to hear this. Even if your son might not have a chance to meet up with his father, but this will allow your child to connect with his father in a good way. Good, now you start practicing again."

"Zhi Yu, you are great! Just like your father, you have many friends," Mei Ru said with a smile.

"Very good, you're on the roll, let's go!"

"Zhi Yu, you are great! Just like your father, you are very helpful," said Mei Ru, finding it getting easier as she continued to practice.

"That's great! When you are back, once you have the chance, you have to start doing that. And it has to come from your heart, your son will definitely be able to feel it; afterward, once you have a chance, do allow your children to interact with their father. It doesn't matter what they learn from their father, as long as there is interaction, they will have a chance to learn some good lessons from their father's life experiences."

The rigidness on Mei Ru's face was gone, she was finally to look at me with a smile.

The next day during my workshop, everyone was discussing what they discovered when they went home and did the homework of "praising the children about their strong points which are similar to their father", one of the ladies excitedly held on to the microphone and said, "It was a miracle, teacher! When I went home and told my son that he was kind like his father, guess what happened? My son volunteered to *help me hang out the clothes to dry! There was a mini commotion as everyone was eager to share their experiences and after the workshop, Mei Ru ran over and thanked me with a smile.*

Letting Go Of The Past And Self Reconciliation

In the two real life examples we featured in this chapter, Liu Fang and Mei Ru's courage were admirable. It is not easy to let go of the past, but for the sake of their children, even though they felt lots of anger when facing their ex-husbands, they were still willing to help their children connect with their fathers. They were willing to diligently focus on the plus points of their exes and learnt to understand the needs of their adolescent children. As a result, the desires of their children were met and more importantly, they were able to find peace and reconciliation in the conflict that has been in their heart for so many years. When we let go of the past, we are freeing ourselves. Even if a couple were to be separated, the two parents should still let their children know that "All the issues between the adults belong to the adults. It has nothing to do with you. Your father will forever be your father. if you love him, become like him or if you want to contact him, I agree." At this moment, the desire in the child's heart will be met and the child no longer feels torn within (Franke, 2003a).

The Principle of Reality: Please Do Not Deny The Identity Of A Child's Parents

Half of a child comes from the father and half of the child comes from their mother. Should we deny either the father or the mother of the child, it would be equivalent to us unconsciously rejecting half of the child; in addition, a child is formed from the cells of his father and mother, and so in the sub conscious mind of every child, is the desire for their parents to be connected. However, just living together is already not an easy feat for a couple and so, how can we expect each and every couple stay together till their old age? Therefore, while it is common to hear of couples separating, the important thing is that when they break up, how do we help the child to face up to this separation? Do we really understand what is going on in the deeper layers of the child's mind?

According to psychologist, Maslow's research, when a person's physiological needs are met, (this means right after they are fed and clothed) their next biggest desire is love and acknowledgement. These are like spiritual foods. Should we be denied of it, we will feel empty and depressed. A child's deepest longing is actually to **feel a deep sense of belonging by being connected to their mother and father**. This supersedes all material desires. So how do children connect with their parents? Just like we mentioned previously, they connect by doing the same things and through taking the same actions which allows the child to feel as if "we are on the same team". This is the desire or the need to belong. Therefore, the child does not really care about the content of what they do. Even if it should require them to go against the Principle, they would still do it. Our deep need to belong is just like our strong need for food in times of extreme hunger. It is a need so strong that even robbing other people to get food becomes an acceptable act.

Therefore, we need to understand the deeper needs of our children (which is their need to connect with both parents). Only then can we fulfill their desire to belong. Should the child not be able to connect to any one of their parents, he or she will feel emptiness and regret. And the thing that a child can least tolerate is for one of the parents to negate, exclude or refuse to acknowledge the other parent. To the child, it would feel as if half of himself is trying to exclude the other half of himself and this will most certainly result in a separation inside his or her mind (Hellinger et al., 1998).

For example, if the mother often talks bad about the father and does not acknowledge the father, in order to connect with the father, the child may take extreme measures. They may do the same things as their father did or may also have the same situations happen to them. Because the child does not have the mother's permission to do so, they will seem to listen to their mother on the surface but become like their father in private. They may even subconsciously follow the life pattern of their father without any self-awareness.

When we refuse to acknowledge our wife or husband, what sort of messages are we sending to our children?

"Your father is lazy and irresponsible; you better don't turn out like him in future!"

"Your father loves to gamble; you better don't indulge in gambling like he did."

"Your father likes to fool around with other women, you must never be like him!"

"Your mother loves money to death, you must never be like her!"

"Your mother is so naggy, you better don't become naggy like her in future!"

"Your mother doesn't care about the family; you must never be like her in future!"

I guarantee that when the children grow up, they will definitely exhibit these behaviours: lazy, irresponsible, have a love for gambling, fools around with women; or, loves money to death, naggy, doesn't care about the family. Why is that so? That is because they have a strong need to connect with their parents but all the information, they have received about their parent is negative. Therefore, they can only connect with this negative information and take on these negative characteristics just so they can fulfill their desire to belong.

When a child's world is filled with only information about laziness, irresponsibility, fooling around with women, loving money to death, love of being naggy, not caring for the family, what other choices does the child have?

Someone told me that they put it all in their hearts and did not vocalize it. If you have these thoughts and information in your mind, you will most certainly display them unconsciously and your children will most definitely feel it too. When a couple negates their partner because of their behaviour and denies their position as a father/mother, the child would naturally behave in the same way as the excluded parent. Simply put, the less you respect your partner, the more your child will be like him/her.

What should we do in that case?

Since it is a child's deepest desire to connect to their parents, then, let's provide lots of positive information for the child to connect with.

"My child, you are great, you are clever just like your father!"

"My child, you are so great, you are loyal just like your father!"

"My child, you are great, you are popular among your friends just like your father!"

"My child, you are so great, you are filial just like your father!"

"My child, you are great, you are kind just like your mother!"

"My child, you are so great, you are caring just like your mother!"

"My child, you are great, you love learning just like your mother!"

"My child, you are so great, you are serious and earnest when you do things, just like your mother!"

Clever, loyal, popular, filial; kind, caring, love to earn and serious and earnest when doing things…

If these information were to fill up our child's world, what direction will our children grow towards?

Therefore, just praising the child is not enough. We have to learn to praise them about the plus points they have inherited from our partners from our hearts. We do not merely praise the child; the important bit is the part where you say they are "just like your father" or "just like mother". When we do this, our children will connect in a positive way with the other parent and their deep longing to belong will be met.

In summary, a child is like the mirror of a family. Just how do we educate, guide and support their growth? Firstly, we have to respect that our other half is the child's father/mother and give permission for the child to connect with them. "If you are like your father, I will be very happy," or "If you are like your mother, I will be very happy."

When a child is allowed to fulfill their need to belong, they will not try to strongly connect with the undesirable traits of the other partner in secret. This is especially the case for divorced parents.

If divorced parents can be aware and do this for their children, their children will definitely develop and grow in a positive direction.

Through their parents, they will also be able to learn that sometimes, adults do quarrel and they might end up separated, but they will still be able to acknowledge each other's position and acknowledge each other's identity as the father or mother of the child. This is one of the most important lessons we could teach by example and it is also a very powerful blessing for the child.

So please remember, never deny your other half's position as a father/mother because of their behaviour because the truth will not change just because you try to hide it. Choosing to deny or hide the truth will only make the child feel that they are being denied too.

Exercise: Praising Your Child In Areas Where He Is Like Your Other Half

Now that we understand what goes on in the deeper layers of our children's minds, let's put it into good practice!

Please write down your husband/wife's three good points. Do not write down what they may not have. That just means we are merely unwilling to think about it and unwilling to see it.

Even the most annoying people will have their plus points. Give it a try!

Please write down the good points of your child where they are like your husband/wife:

    1.

    2.

    3.

Next, put them into the following sentences and practice them:

"_____ (Child's name), you are great, like your father, you are _____ (plus point)!"

"_____ (Child's name), you are great, like your mother, you are _____ (plus point)!"

Remember that during your daily life, find a suitable time to put this into practice. For example, if your child exhibits the above-mentioned behaviour, you could use the above-mentioned sentences to praise them. I firmly believe that after we do this over an extended period, the child will most certainly develop and grow in this direction!

Leaves Drop So That New Shoots Can Grow- Teaching Children To Face Death

If we can totally face up the grief we have when we lose a loved one, we allow the grieving process to complete. Not only is this healthy, it will give our life a new energy to move forward (Shih, 2008).

Kevin is from Singapore and is in his early forties. He mentioned that he is worried because his son tends to have many sudden, unexplained emotions.

"My son constantly suffers from insomnia and nightmares and will often say many shocking things. For example, my son cried out loud in his sleep one night during his nightmares and when I ran over to see how he was, he said to me, "Father, I thought you died!""

I asked Kevin, "So who is the person who really died?"

Just a simple sentence from this 12-year-old boy brought Kevin back to all the sadness that he had. His son's nightmare made him remember something that happened in his childhood and a fear that he has been unable to shake off—a fear of parting forever in death.

"Back then, I was only 12. The moment I woke up, I had lost my father. My father had a sudden heart attack and died just like that."

The night before, Kevin had still been interacting with these beloved kin and just after a single night, they will never be able to interact with each other again. As Kevin was sharing his story, his body started to tremble. He started to choke in tears as he talked about his fears and pain. The death of his father planted a seed of fear of loss in his heart. Since young, he has always been worrying about the people he loves passing on suddenly even though this has never happened again. And of course, his son's reaction out of nowhere stems from an unconscious desire to help Kevin shoulder this fear.

I continued to explain, "If your grief towards losing your father was deep enough, after some time, it will pass. But if you did not grief over it, the grief will always stay there and the whole family will be shadowed by death and your children will feel it and live in fear of separation through death."

"Yes, you are right. I feel very tired and wish to relax but somehow, I am never able to truly relax. I constantly accept new jobs and it feels as if I am trying to run away from something by working very hard."

"Running away is only a temporary strategy. If we do not face the root of the issue, part of your life energy will be frozen in the past. This unfinished business in your family will present itself through your child.

For the sake of his son, Kevin decided to face up to the issue.

I invited one of the participants to lie down on the floor to represent Kevin's father. I also got another two people to represent Kevin's mother and his son. They stood by the side and as for Kevin, I got him to face the issue himself.

But facing up to the issue is easier said than done.

Kevin held on to his son's hands and his other hand was pressed over his chest. He was breathing rapidly and his eyes were red. Looking at his father who is lying dead on the floor, he seemed frozen and unable to move.

On the other hand, Kevin's mother never once looked in the direction of Kevin's father. Kevin's father who passed away was lying on the floor but his eyes remain opened.

"If those who are alive are unable to let go, the people who are dead will never be able to pass on in peace!" Like an alarm, I woke both Kevin and his mother from their "trance".

Yes, the deepest love will often get frozen and be unable to melt and flow. Sometimes it is because people want to possess it, sometimes it is because of shock, (as is the case in Kevin's family) and thus, they are unable to let go. Obviously in this case, Kevin, his mother and his father were not ready to let go. Kevin kept crying as he looked at his father while his mother looked helpless in her pain. This sort of entanglement will mean that his deceased father will be unable to pass on in peace!

I got Kevin's mother to say to her husband who is still unable to close his eyes. "My dear, you are already dead." His mother closed her eyes and started to cry.

It is painful to face the truth but for the sake of the peace of those who are still alive and those who have passed on, it is important for us to face up to it no matter how difficult it may be. Kevin moved forward to accompany his mother and to face up to this together. And now that they can rely on each other, they found renewed strength and kneeled down together in front of the deceased to face their grief.

"Dear, you are already dead..." both of the started to cry.

When we recognize the truth, the real grief will start. In the gush of sadness, both mother and son hugged the father tightly and wailed. They were shivering all over and the sound of their cries was accompanied by real grief. His father's frozen face started to relax and finally, he closed both of his eyes in peace.

And just like that, their grief started to flow forward. I gave them some space to express the sadness and grief that they feel.

After some time, the sounds of their cry seem to calm down a little.

I told Kevin, "Tell your father about your current situation and ask him not to worry and rest in peace."

"Father, I am married and am now in my forties. I have a son and we are very well. Please do not worry. Mother is very well. Please do not worry. Please bless us and bless your grandchild that he may grow up happy and healthy."

A peaceful smile appeared on his father's face. Both his eyes are closed and everyone in the family is finally at peace.

"If we keep holding on to the dried leaves of autumn and cry in sadness, we will be unable to see the young shoots that spring brings. However, life continues to move on in cycles and it will continue to go on and on," I was inspired to encourage them.

Life is a constant, never-ending cycle. The power of a father and mother's love is also passed down from generation to generation. Now, with a happy smile, Kevin is able to commit both to himself and his child, "Child, you don't have to be afraid anymore. Father will live on well and I will allow myself to live on happily!"

Children Inherit All Unfinished Business And Emotions In The Family

It takes a lot of courage to face up to all the pain we have accumulated over the years in our hearts. Some people may not want to or dare to face up to them during their entire lives. But for the sake our children, we will be willing to do anything and that is the greatness of a father or mother's love. Kevin's courage was admirable. But we have to also understand the psychological foundation behind it before we can apply it with awareness in our lives. A family is a system and like an organism, the influence of other members in the system is often so big it is beyond what we can possibly imagine; if there are unfinished businesses in the family, the unfinished emotions will be taken on by the members within the system, especially children who have the lowest immunity. Therefore, our children are like the family's mirror. All these unfinished businesses will be "reflected" in our children (Hellinger, 2001a). If the children have any abnormal, unexplainable emotions, special reactions, behaviours or symptoms, that is often a reminder to take a good look at what the child is trying to say. Are there any hidden messages in the family system? Are there hidden dynamics, people who were excluded or any unfinished businesses waiting for us to face?

At the same time, it is important to understand that every family system has their own driving force that tries to bring things to completion and every family system has the ability to self-adjust. Therefore, our children's reactions are actually a form of motivation to urge this family to complete this unfinished business so that it can grow in a better direction. Therefore, we can use these diagnosis and family incidents as good learning tools for our children.

Principle of Flow: Facing Family Pain

The most often occurrence of an "unfinished business" is usually in the form of some sort of sudden trauma. A "trauma" is a very personal experience and people relate to it differently. Take the example of sudden catastrophes and accidents like the Sichuan Earthquake and Taiwan's 921 Earthquake. During those times, some people continue to feel fear even after the earthquakes are over. But some recover from it after a short while. For those people who still feel a lot of fear even though the trauma has been over for some time, they have what psychologists' term as Post Traumatic Stress Disorder (PTSD) (Chun, 1998).

I discovered that some traumas involve the whole family. I call it a "Family Trauma". When a family member passes away suddenly as a result of an accident or a sudden chronic illness, the whole family immediately goes into shock. Because it is too sudden, the family members do not know what to do or how to react. Therefore, the life force of the family becomes frozen together with the love they have for this person.

How will this affect us? Levine (2005) discovered that part of our life force is frozen at the age where the incident happened and so, without 100% of our life force, we are unable to live life to the fullest. Usually, the person who is in such a situation will be unaware of this but will somehow subconsciously have many unexplainable emotions, accidents, illnesses or failures. Sometimes, they may even unconsciously walk towards death without being aware of it; in more serious cases, if the generation of family members who are facing the issue do not face up to the issue or take time to grieve over it properly, this suppressed emotion will become a hidden dynamic in the family and may continue to affect even the third or the fourth generation. Even though the future generations may not have gone through the trauma themselves, they will continue to feel the same emotions or behave in the same way as those who did, as if they have also contracted the post-traumatic stress disorder too. This is the reason why children in families with family trauma will tend to exhibit unexplainable behaviours (Drugge, 2008).

How do we heal this trauma?

We can only heal it through love. Only when our love starts flowing will our life also start to move in a flow.

But if our loved ones have already passed on, how do we face up to that?

If our loved one has already passed on but we have yet to resolve the sadness in our hearts, this sadness will continue on in the sub conscious mind of the family system. Systemic Constellations can help us heal this trauma. The way to do it is through the representatives in the constellations. We invite someone who is experienced in this area to represent the person who has passed on and let him or her lie down on the floor. We can kneel or sit beside this person representing our loved one and if possible, I suggest that the children take part in this process as well and kneel down beside this person. The whole family will then get a chance to face their grief and say their farewells one more time. When we do this, we create a new physical experience and a new mental image in our minds. By doing this, we allow this expression of grief to become an experience of expressing of our deepest emotions. The whole process is usually very touching and memorable. It can help us melt all the frozen knots in our hearts and allow the (frozen) love and life force to go back into the flow again (Levine, 2005).

When we can stand in our rightful position in the family system and accept all the unpredictable changes of life, our loved ones who have passed on will be able to find peace and be happy to see that we respect their fates and choose to live well continually. Not only are we not beaten by life's surprises, we actually overcome it and lead even better, happier lives. When our ancestors see this, they will naturally be happy to bless the future generations. More importantly, our children will no longer need to carry the burden of these unfinished businesses. They can also learn how to face up to the irregularities of life from us and welcome in into their lives, a newfound power from living in the present.

Inner Constellation: Blessings For Family Members Who Have Suddenly Passed On

Are you ready to go back into your position in the family system and let your loved ones who have passed away find peace? Please remember to do the exercise within the parameters of emotions that are acceptable to you and complete it slowly with love:

Please sit upright
Let your both feet touch the ground
Feel the support of the earth
Use your heart and take a good look at some people in our family
Those who have passed away suddenly in our family
Regardless of whether it is an accident or a suicide
As long as it is someone that you can see in your heart now

If you still haven't thought of anyone
That's ok as well
You just need to imagine
That right in front of us
Are the people in the past few generations of our family
Who have passed away in tragedy
Or anyone who appears in our heart
Right at this present moment
Their death
Is something we are unwilling to face up
And unable to let go

And unable to leave behind

Now, please take a good look at them
With a little bit of love
Take a long look at them
And then tell them

"I can see you now
I can see you now
Regardless of the mishaps that might have happened to you
I respect whatever has happened to you
I respect your destiny
You will always have a place in my heart
I will pass on
The love you have for us
From you
I will learn the lessons that life brings
All the more I will also treasure my life
And use this life to do some things
So that your spirit
May be passed on
So that your death is not in vain
Please rest in peace"

Now, please use your own way to show your respect
You can give a bow or you can kowtow to him or her
Use a way that is relevant to your relationship to show respect
When you come back, remember to bring along their blessings with you
Stand up with your back straight slowly
Take a step backwards
And return to your position

Family Black Holes-
The Source Of Undesirable Behaviour In Children

Hellinger (2001a) discovered that we cannot just look at the surface of our children's actions and have to also understand the deeper messages these actions may have for the family. For example, if someone in the family system is excluded, a black hole will be created in the family, and the child will be affected by this black hole and produce various inappropriate behaviors.

Liang Cheng and Mei Yu are a pair of conscientious parents who are constantly learning. Because of their child, Ren Yao's problem, they have been seeking all sorts of help and attending all sorts of workshops.

Even though Ren Yao is only a high school student, he gambles, mixes with the gangsters and borrows money without repaying. His parents are very worried and hope that his deviant behaviour will improve. Once when I was invited to conduct a workshop in Hualien (Taiwan), they brought their son, Ren Yao, to my workshop.

I invited the three of them to sit in the front and Ren Yao very unwillingly followed his parents to the front. He crossed his arms and put one of his ankles over the other thigh and had a cocky look on his face. It was as if he was saying with his body language, "I don't give a dam about what you adults are up to!"

"Sigh... He is always like this," says his mother.

"He gambles in school and mixes with the wrong crowd," echoed his dad while glaring at him.

"Do you or your wife gamble at home?" I asked.

"No, both of us do not gamble at all."

"So your child did not learn gambling from the both of you."

"Yes, and we are so worried about him. We have done all we could but this child is still like this."

"Okay, let's take a look at what the child's actions are trying to say."

I invited three people to represent the father, mother and Ren Yao and got Liang Cheng and Meiyu to place their representatives in the constellations to reflect their relationship. But something very interesting happened. The representative who was representing Ren Yao had the same posture as the real Ren Yao. He had his arms crossed and he was shaking his leg with a look of cockiness on his face, just like a carbon copy. The representative was not trying to imitate Ren Yao but his posture was his body's natural reaction in his role.

Also, even though his parents are beside him, it seems that Ren Yao does not pay them much attention but seemed attracted by some unknown force in force of him.

"Did anything happen in your family? For example, was there anyone who was being excluded?"

Liang Cheng and Mei Yu thought for a while and shook their heads.

All of a sudden, Mei Yu recalled something. "I have a brother, Ren Yao's uncle, who often borrowed money to gamble and mixes with the triads. He borrowed lots of money from the family and never repaid any of his debts. Therefore, everyone in the family hated him to the core and wanted to sever our ties with him so that we could exclude him from our family."

I thought this uncle might have something to do with it. "Okay, let's give it a try."

I asked Mei Yu to choose someone to represent her brother and place him inside the constellations. Without any instruction from anyone,

Mei Yu placed her brother in a far corner of the classroom, far away from everyone else.

At this moment, the hidden truth in the family revealed itself. Ren Yao was very much attracted by this uncle and kept walking towards him to be closer to him. Eventually, he moved right next to his uncle and stood beside him, as if they are on very close terms.

Mei Yu was very puzzled, "Ren Yao and his uncle were not very familiar with each other. Why does he stand so close to him?"

"Yes, and this is what I have observed from thousands of families. From this constellations, we can see that hidden influences in your family come from the fact that your family has excluded your brother from his position in your family. It is as if you have created a black hole in your family system and your son is attracted to the black hole and wants to fill it up by modeling after his uncle."

"Do you mean to say that Ren Yao's behaviour is linked to his uncle? Isn't that a little strange?"

"It is normal for you to think this way since the education we have received is mostly based on material science. Thus, most people have little knowledge about psychology. But this is a proven psychological theory and has been proven by thousands of examples all over the world."

"Can you tell me what theory this is?"

"This is the 'Principle of Order', it means that our family is actually a system and everyone in the family has a position they belong to inside the system; regardless of their behaviours or what has happened, they will forever have a place in this family system. But your brother was excluded from the family and this went against the 'Principle of Order'."

"When people belonging to our family system are excluded, it will create a black hole and other members of the family will desire to fill it up to replace this person's position and unconsciously acknowledge them by repeating their life patterns and stories. This means that as a result of your brother being excluded from his position in the family, a black hole is being created and it is attracting your son try to fill it up. That is why your son has the same behavioural model as your brother."

Mei Yu looked at me doubtfully.

"You don't have to believe me. I am just sharing with you what I observed. This has already helped thousands of people all over the world but you will have to experience it for yourself to understand it."

"So, what should I do?"

"You need to change your attitude towards your brother. This will be the key to resolving this problem."

When she heard the words "key to resolving the problem", Mei Yu suddenly became very interested as they have been disturbed by this problem for a long, long time.

"I am willing to give it a try no matter what."

"Just trying is not enough, you will have to change your attitude from the bottom of your heart for this to work. Are you willing to do that?"

"Yes, I am willing," Mei Yu nodded her head.

I invited Mei Yu herself to stand in front of her brother's representative.

"Now, you have to apologize to your brother."

"What! Apologize?" Mei Yu exclaimed. "He is the one who did not repay the money I lent him. Why should I apologize to him?"

When Mei Yu reacted in this way, her brother's representative started to stepped even further away. Her son, Ren Yao, continued to stand beside his uncle and moved far, far away.

"See for yourself! When you exclude your brother, your son will follow him and repeat his actions and move further and further away from you!"

Mei Yu was in shock. It was difficult to accept the truth before her eyes.

"Then what should I do?"

I explained to her, "Apologize to your brother. I am not asking you to agree to his behaviour of not repaying his debts. But you have to apologize for excluding him from the family. You have reaccept him as your brother in heart so that he has a place in the family once more."

Mei Yu seems to be starting to understand what all this is about and slowly comprehend the logic behind it.

"I asked you not to gamble but you refused to listen. We do not want these things to happen to you. Now that you are in this sorry state and running away from hour debtors, we also tried to help you repay some of your debt... Dad and Mum are so sad to see you in this situation...'

I guided Mei Yu, "I do not wish for these things to happen to you and you have to be responsible for your own actions but I have to let you know, that regardless of what happened, you are always my brother and you will always be a part of our family. We all hope that you will lead a good life."

Right after she finished, Mei Yu started to cry. After all, they are one family and she still loves her brother.

"I am sorry, brother. I am sorry. Now I will give you a place in my heart again, you will forever be my younger brother."

At this moment, some changes came about in the representative representing her brother. He started to walk closer to his sister and he moved closer and closer, closer and closer, till he was finally in front of his sister and he gave his sister a small bow.

Mei Yu held her brother's hands, here eyes were filled with tears and her voice filled with emotion, "You will forever be a part of our family, I really hope that you will have a good life."

When her brother was once again accepted by Mei Yu, her son, Ren Yao's representative also started to walk closer towards his father and finally moved into the child's position right beside his father. Following that, something even more miraculous happened. The real Ren Yao, who had been crossing his arm and shaking his half crossed leg suddenly uncrossed his arms and put both feet on the floor. He sat up straight and started to look like a youthful high school student again. There was a faint smile on his lips. He looked like a totally different person.

Everyone in the workshop was surprised by his change.

In actual fact, there is nothing miraculous about this so long as we return to our own positions and respect everybody's position in the family. When a child does not need to take the place of another adult, he or she will be able to be himself or herself again.

Principle of Wholeness And Order: Unraveling Entanglements

In the above-mentioned real-life example, we can once again witness the power of the Principle of Order and Principle of Wholeness and how they work.

Let us do a quick revision. What is the "Principle of Wholeness" and the "Principle of Order"?

The "Principle of Wholeness" refers to this: everyone in the family has a place or position that belongs to them and will forever have this "place" regardless or what they have done or what may have happened. But very often, we would exclude some of our family members because their behaviour did not meet the family's expectations. For example, they may gamble, become alcoholic, commit a crime, etc. Another more common reason for exclusion would be that something unacceptable happened to him or her (they may be still born, commit suicide or died in an accident) and therefore, we try to unconsciously forget or exclude this person as if they don't have any place in this family. But all these go against the Principle that states that every part of the system has to have a place they belong to. The price to pay for that would be inexplicable emotions, behaviour, repeated tragedy and in extreme cases, separation with the family or even death of the whole family. Even though the influence of this Principle is so extensive, it is very often neglected by us (Franke, 2003a).

The "Principle of Order" is referring to how there is a sequential order (based on seniority) in the family just like the traditional Chinese concept of "being respectful towards your elder siblings, friends and younger siblings based on seniority." The juniors have to respect their elders, and the elders have to love and protect the juniors. This is a truth that everyone knows.

Now, from Liang Chen and Mei Yu's example, we can see how "Wholeness" and "Order" work together. Both principles include considerations towards "sequential order" and also "position". This means that within the family system, everyone is given a position based on the sequential order that they join this family system and as long as you have a position, you have the right to belong to this system.

I often use this concept as an analogy: our family is like a mini universe. The solar system is a big universe. In the family of the solar system, there are 9 planets. Every planet has a position, just like how everyone has their own position in the family system. Imagine this, if one of the planets were to be removed or excluded, this means that a black hole is created. The whole solar system will try to fill up this black hole to regain balance. But this will cause every planet in the solar system to have big changes in their orbiting paths. In serious cases, they might even collide and destroy each other.

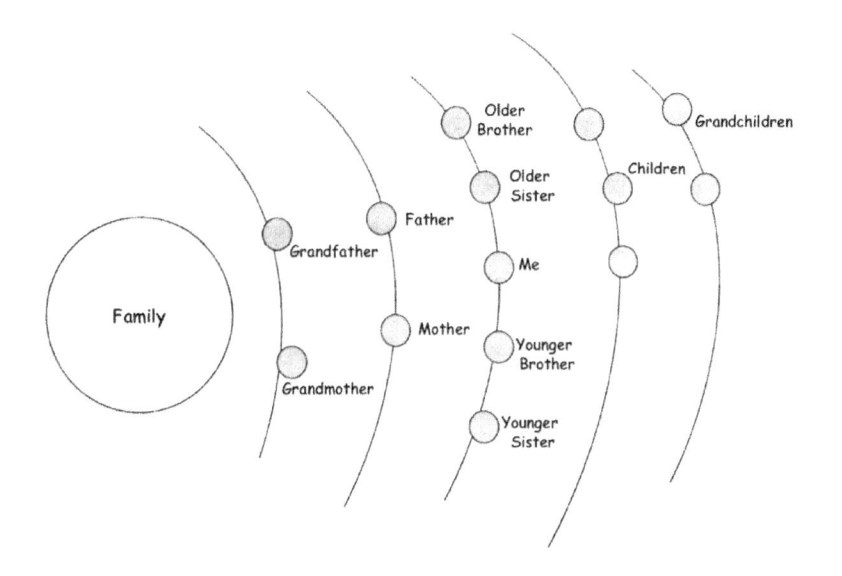

Figure 2: Using the solar system to explain how a family system works

By the same logic, everyone in the family system will need a place that belongs to them. If their place is being removed, sometimes this creates a black hole and other family members will be attracted by it and try fill it up. That means they will leave their orbiting path and try to replace the person who is excluded so as to unconsciously acknowledge this person by repeating their behaviour or life patterns. Hellinger termed this phenomenon as "**entanglement**' (Helllinger et al., 1998).

One example of this is a case where a mother came to me for help. She could not acknowledge her husband, because her husband had raped her and caused her to give birth to her son. But the mother does not want her child to know that his father is a rapist and naturally, this means that the father's position is being denied and excluded from this family system. In the father's position is a black hole. Make a guess what happened? When the child grew up, he was also on the verge of becoming a rapist and it was only then that the mother realized that even though the way she educated her son was to exclude and deny his father, the end result is that the son ended up behaving like his father. This is a very obvious case of the above stated.

Therefore, the next important point is, who belongs to our family system? Because, just like the solar system, these are the people who will guide us along and share the burden of the family's destiny.

Who Belongs To My Family System

Hellinger (2001a) discovered that not every relative belongs to our family system. Only a group of specific people belong to our system and these are the group of people who will create entanglements in our lives. This group of people includes the people who are related to us by blood and people who are not blood related. In this chapter, we will talk only about blood relations and I will talk about the non-blood relations in the next chapter.

Our blood relations include: our children, ourselves, our siblings and our parents and their siblings (our aunts and uncles). It also includes our paternal grandparents, maternal grandparents and sometimes, even one or two great grandparents. All these people belong to our system whether they are alive or dead. Only when all the places in the system are filled will the system be whole.

We can imagine that the above-mentioned people are like planets orbiting within the solar system. They definitely need a place in the system so that the family can operate in balance. However, we often have blind spots, for example a family member may die and we may neglect them or if someone does something that is bad for the reputation for the family, we may deny or exclude them in our hearts. This means that he or she will no longer have a place in the system and thus, this will create an imbalance within the system.

Therefore, our affinity gives us a chance to become a family with these people. So, we have to learn from these relationships. We have to learn respect, balance, wholeness, how to interact with our family members, how to give everyone a place in our heart and how to do a little something for our deceased family members, so on and so forth.

Therefore, the rites involving special prayers to our ancestors and ancestral blessings have got sound logic behind it. Based on Principles of Relationships, we can see that having prayers for our ancestors is also a way of paying respect to the elders/seniors in the system. Even though the family might bring about entanglements, it might also bring about support and blessings. These principles regarding "wholeness" and "order" in a system are in fact congruent with Chinese Confucian teachings and are helping us move towards are more harmonious, whole relationship. If we respect and understand this Principle from the bottom of our hearts, the family system will be able to offer support and blessings and we can bring a certain fulfillment and completion to our affinity with these family members.

Homework: Returning To Your Roots, Drawing Your Family System Chart

Now that we know who are the blood relations who belong to our family system, the following is a very important piece of homework that might help us find our position and complete the family system's affinity. We are not only doing this for ourselves but also for our family members. Now, please follow the steps below and start your journey to search for your roots!

Step 1, Draw out your family system chart: Please use a piece of paper and draw out all your family members in the family tree. List out everybody's identity and their position. Just draw and include anything and everything you know.

Step 2, Understand your family stories: include the incidents that you know and write them down beside the respective people.

The following 10 questions will help to provide clues and they are some of the information you might need to know in advance before you start a family constellations process. Please find out about the following with regards to you and your parents:

1. Did anyone in the family pass away at a young age?

2. When they were young, did anyone around your parents pass away?
3. Was anyone in the family given away, adopted or considered illegitimate?
4. Are your parents each other's first relationship? (Have they every been married, engaged or have had intimate relationships with other people)
5. Ever had a miscarriage or an abortion
6. Family secrets (for example, is there anyone being excluded? Is there any family wealth that was unevenly distributed or any ill gotten gains)
7. Criminal activities (for example murder, being murdered or violence)
8. Any chronic diseases in the family or any disabilities or addictions (eg, drug abuse, alcoholic, gambling)
9. Has anyone in the family had a mental problem, committed suicide or turned violent
10. Migration

Please write down the above stories and information under the respective family members in your family tree.

Step 3, Give them a place in your heart: Look at your family system chart and give everyone in the family a place in your heart and give them your blessings. You have to do it sincerely from your heart and you can start by doing one family member a day. Very, very slowly, give them a bow. The slower the better and give them a place in your heart.

Step 4, To be added on in future: When there is a suitable chance, during your family gatherings, find out about your family history from your parents and your grandparents. Understand who are the people in your family, which of the people have unique lifestyles and may have what sort of special incidents happening to them. Add these to your family system chart and give them a place in your heart.

Please keep this family system chart with you. In the next chapter, we will add in the non-blood related members in the family system into this same chart so that the chart of your family system will be more complete.

(Refer to Figure 3: Chart Featuring Blood Relations In The Family System)

168

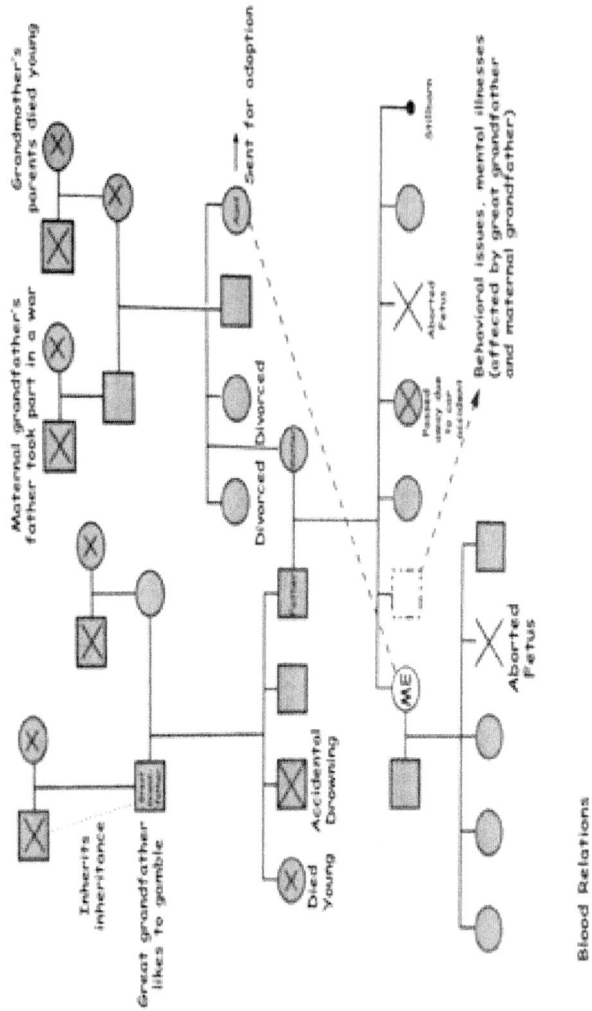

Chapter 5: Sibling & Other Family Relationships

If you don't believe me, see for yourself! The more a person is not ethical or moral, for example, if a parent is not kind to their children, if children are not filial to their parents, if the older siblings are not friendly with each other, if younger siblings are not respectful towards each other or if friends do not trust each other, the more they will suffer from hardships in future and not be able to enjoy happiness. They are definitely going to worry about never ending troubles!

--Wang Feng Yi (Chinese enlightened peasant in the 1950s)

不信你看看吧！越是不盡倫常道的人，如父母不慈，子女不孝，兄姐不友，弟妹不恭，朋友不信，將來越吃苦受罪，沒有福享，準是苦惱無邊啊！

　　--王鳳儀（民初開悟農民）

Family: A Common Destiny

The Great Philosopher and Educator of China, Confucius, compared our families to our bodies. Every person in the family is like our different body parts which make up our whole body and cannot be separated: The relationship between father and son is like the relationship between our head and our legs, husband and wife are different parts of the body and brothers are like the hands and legs. Therefore, the connection between the family members is tight. Just like the different body parts in our body system, all the different parts of the family system share the same destiny (Lee, 2021).

But, why do siblings and relatives fall out with each other?

Based on my umpteen years of observations made with tens and thousands of families, I have categorized the reasons under 3 main categories:

1. **First reason would be a disorder within the family:** When our relatives or siblings lose respect for our elders or are not kind and loving to the young, or when people who should have a rightful position in the family are excluded, forgotten or neglected, there will be some amount of disorder in the family.

2. **Second reason would be money disputes:** When the family has some form of monetary imbalance with other family members or other people or has a part in some ill gotten gains, it will create a cause for money disputes.

3. **Third reason would be the aftermath influence of any murder or incident related to killing:** When someone in the family commits murder, is being murdered or being harmed and the incident has not received reconciliation yet, it will result in disputes and disharmony between siblings.

The above mentioned examples are applicable in both Chinese and Western families and most people only finally understand the depth of its influence at the point where they pay a painful price for it.

So how do we increase our awareness about this quickly? We have to search amongst the wisdom of our ancestors and apply it appropriately together with Principles of Relationships. In addition, we have to learn from our life stories and the stories of the people around us.

Jiang (2001) summarized that in the past 5000 years, China has seen millions of family problems and therefore our forefathers have long learnt their lesson and have come up with a wise saying about it: "The elder sibling should show the younger family members friendly love. And the younger ones should show respect. I will behave well with my brothers and sisters because I love and respect my parent. If everyone values harmony above possession then resentment is avoided. If everyone is careful with their choice of words then upsets are quickly resolved." （兄道友，弟道恭，兄弟睦，孝在中，財物輕，怨何生，言語忍，忿自泯。） The spirit behind this saying is actually the same as the conclusion that we have arrived based on our observations and research with thousands of families. Therefore, the earlier we learn from the wisdom of our forefathers, the earlier we master the Principles of Relationships. When we understand this with our hearts and apply it, we will be able to weaken the family disputes and disharmony.

Based of the conventional wisdom of the east and the use of western psychology methods such as Systemic Constellations, I have observed that other than our blood relations, there are other "non blood related" people who will affect the fate of our family system. The effect that these people have on us is similar to that of our family members. In some cases, the effects may actually be even more far reaching than compared to the influence of our family members. And just as the analogy that Confucius used, these people are also like a part of our body system and will share the same fate as we do.

You Are One Of Us-
Order Amongst Siblings

All of you are dead but I am still alive—the survivor often has to overcome a special type of guilt to allow them to lead happy lives, so that they can share the happiness with their siblings who have passed away (Hsu, 2012).

Zi Tong from Taipei is a pediatrician. A respected physician, even though she has accumulated huge amounts of knowledge in the medical area and is very experienced, she is still humble and keeps on learning. She attended my personal growth classes in order to have a deeper understanding of Systemic Constellations.

During one of our sessions, I was talking about relationship between siblings. The usually quiet and reserved Zi Tong actually volunteered and fought for the chance to be the example person in the class demonstration.

I looked at Zi Tong, unlike her usual self, she looked a little lost as if she did not know what to do. Both her fists are clenched tightly into a ball and I could tell she was very nervous. I smiled at her and she tried her best to smile back.

"What do we want to talk about today?"

"Including me, there are 4 brothers and sisters in my family but our relationship with each other is very distant," she continued to seem nervous as she tried to describe her situation.

"Based on my experience, I feel you do not only have 4 brothers and sisters in your family," I replied.

I looked at Zi Tong and repeated assuredly, "You do not only have 4 brothers and sisters in your family.

The whole room fell into silence.

After a while, Zi Tong started to share her story, "My father's first wife had three children. The eldest boy passed away within a week after he was born. Then they had two twins but because of complications with the labour, both the twins and their mother passed away. Thereafter, my father remarried my mother and gave birth to four children. I have two elder sisters, followed by a brother and I am the youngest."

"Oh, so if I add on the siblings being born by your father and his first wife, you actually have 7 siblings in total! Even though all these three children have already passed away with your dad's first wife, they are still your siblings."

After listening to this story, we can now understand why Zi Tong chose to be a doctor, and a pediatrician as such. Her elder brother is also a doctor. This shows us how unconsciously we will like to share the burden of our family, even to the extent of having it affecting our career choice.

I asked her, "Your brother feels a lot of pressure. Does he often feel like leaving the house?"

Zi Tong nodded her head and agreed silently. When she opened her mouth again, Zi Tong gradually said, "We live in Taipei and my brother lives in Tainan. We do not meet up often."

"Your brother is the sole surviving male child, I can imagine how much burden he has been taking on from the family."

It goes without saying that all the 4 surviving children will be filled with some invisible pressure in their hearts. The pressure seems to be saying, "You are dead but I have survived." This voice echoes throughout the subconscious information field of all the four children. Unconsciously, they have not dared to allow themselves to live too happily and each of them will more or less experience some amount of guilt. This guilt comes from the people who have been neglected in the family who have not been acknowledged as part of the family, or not properly accepted such as the family members who have passed on.

Therefore, I guided Zi Tong to face them again.

I invited 6 workshop participants to represent Zi Tong's 6 other siblings. Even though it was the first time that Zi Tong got to meet her 3 deceased brother and sisters, somehow, she feels a sense of connection with them. Her face turned slightly pale and she looked a little depressed.

I asked Zi Tong to introduce herself to them. "You are my eldest brother and older sisters. Unfortunately, you did not get to survive I am your youngest sister.

Zi Tong's eyes turned red as she turned to face her deceased eldest brother. Once again, she brought her awareness to his existence and acknowledged his position in the family, "Brother, you are my eldest brother. You are the eldest."

It was heart wrenching for the two siblings to meet for the first time ever. Even though he was only on earth for less than a week, he was in actual fact, still her eldest brother.

Following that, she turned towards the two twin sisters and aunty (in Chinese, one's father's first wife is called 大妈, loosely translated to English, it means something like 'Big/First Mother'.) who died in labour, "Aunty, you are all dead, my two sisters are also dead. This is something really sad…"

"Dear sisters, it is a pity that you did not manage to survive." Zi Tong said as tears flowed out non stop while she held on to her sisters' hands.

At this point, I interjected, "Originally, a pregnancy is a happy occasion where people celebrate. In the end, it became a funeral. This is such a tragedy. I think your father must have been very sad and been in much pain, especially since he is the one standing at the frontline and facing it firsthand.

So I invited another 3 persons to represent Zi Tong's father, mother and aunty, so that they can face the tragedy together.

Her dad was so sad he and he was kneeling down and stroking his deceased wife, it was as if he was blaming himself. All the suppressed sadness gushed out at this moment, "Ai!"

At this moment, his wordless tears say far more than a thousand words.

His deep grief had once again given this unmentionable tragedy the respect it needed; at the same time, with the help of Systemic Constellations, this family finally gets a chance to release the suppressed grief related to the incident that has been bottled up for the past umpteen years.

Following that, the father introduced his deceased wife and children to his current wife. "This is my ex wife, these are our children. They are all dead."

Following that, Zi Tong's mother turned towards her husband's deceased wife. Filled with emotion and sincerity, she said, "I am your husband's second wife. You came before me. If you did not pass away, I would not be together with my husband; if you did not leave, I would not be in this family. It was a great pity you did not survive and I can see your great misfortune, I will do some good deeds to remember you by."

At this moment, the first wife's eyes were finally closed in peace and there were some changes in the siblings that had survived.

Originally, Zi Tong's brother's life force looked as if it was slowly weakening with the loss of the deceased siblings. We could observe that his shoulders seem to be carrying a larger burden than his other three sisters who are alive and there did not seem to be any interaction between the 4 siblings; at this moment, I guided Zi Tong to shout out to her brother with deep feeling, "Brother, thank you for also seeing them, please continue to live on well. Let us do some good deeds for our siblings to remember them."

When he heard Zi Tong's words, her brother started to walk slowly towards her. Hope started to flash in his eyes. It seemed that he had moved further away from the helplessness that he was feeling previously. At the same time, the two sisters unanimously decided to walk closer. For the first time, the 4 siblings were in sync with each other. With tears in their eyes, the four of them formed a circle. Holding on to each other's hands, they faced all their deceased siblings together. And only when they are all willing to face these siblings can they bring cohesion into their estranged relationship.

Finally, the 7 siblings are reunited!

I told Zi Tong, "Put this picture of reunion into your heart and don't be in a hurry to do anything. When your heart feels like doing anything, just do it naturally. By that time, it will become your strength. At the same time, find a suitable chance to chat with your father about his feelings towards his ex wife and do some good things together with him for your deceased siblings."

Within less than 2 months, Zi Tong was back for another workshop. She shared happily that she has started to do some good things for her deceased aunty and siblings and the relationship between her other siblings has improved. It seems easier for them to communicate with each other and they seem to have much more to talk about.

That's great! Keep up the good work!

Disorder Creates Distance Amongst Siblings

Why do siblings become distanced and estranged, why do they fall out with each other? The most common reason would be that they are not in their own position in the correct order (Hellinger et al., 1998).

For example, if they thought that the elder brother who is alive is the eldest son but he actually isn't, then the actual eldest son will not be respected and his position is actually taken up by his younger brother. Therefore there is disorder in the sequential order of the siblings.

From Zi Tong's example, we can see that even though the children are born of a different mother (but of the same father) and even if they passed away at birth, they also ought to have a position belonging to them in the family. This is the "Principle or Order" that we have been emphasizing on. Errors in the order of the siblings go against the "Principle or Order" and thus, the end result is the siblings will either become estranged or may fall out with each other.

From this, we can see that the "Principle of Order" is omnipresent.

The Effect Of Losing Your Siblings

Hellinger (2001a) discovered that when our siblings pass away- even if they passed on due to a miscarriage or passed away when they were young- the siblings who are alive will unconsciously feel a sense of guilt, because they feel that they have received more, their parents have given them more love and care and given their deceased siblings less love and care. And so, they would naturally want to balance it out by compensating for it. However, these actions of compensation are unconscious and there are two directions this could go: Firstly, it could go in a negative direction. They might allow themselves to fail and be unhappy, as if they are telling their deceased sibling, "I am also not living a good life, so I don't have to feel this guilt. We are even." But unfortunately, this sort of compensation is not helpful at all and is actually a form of insult to their deceased siblings.

The other direction this could go would be the positive one. Just as in Zi Tong's example, the siblings who survived became doctors and helped even more people. Even though they did not know why they became doctors, but they were all unconsciously moving towards this direction. This is something good but the problem is, **this is an unconscious compensation** and because they are not aware that this dynamic is the driving force, they might work too hard, do too much and deplete their energies excessively (Hsu, 2012).

Whenever our siblings pass on and are not acknowledged, the siblings who survived will end up trying to do too much. This is because they may unconsciously want to do something extra and work an extra job for their deceased siblings. They work so hard and are yet unaware that they are giving themselves so much pressure that they are almost unable to breathe. However, if we are conscious about what we are doing and bring awareness and love into it, and if we do it in a way where we can remember our deceased siblings and their positions, we will be able to feel a sense of wholeness within and our lives will become healthier and more balanced.

So ,Zi Tong has finally recognised why she has become a Doctor. When she helped a child by putting him to cure. she could tell her deceased siblings and parents in her heart: "I will share all my happiness and reward you all by my good deeds." the compensation for the sense of guilty within Zi Tong would be transformed into a great healing of love.

The Effect Of The Former Partners (The Exes,Ex-husbands, Ex Wives And Ex Partners)

In addition, Systemic Constellations has made an important discovery that has contributed greatly to the application of modern psychology. Hellinger (2001b) has discovered the effects that ex-husbands, ex-wives and former partners have on the second marriage and their children. We have to understand this important truth: The separation with or the death of the former partner make it possibile for the second wife/partner to appear and exist in this family system; and that means because the first wife has actually give her place to the second wife, it has made the second marriage and the birth of their children is possible.

If they did not "make room for the later partner", the future generation will not be born. Therefore, this ex-wife/husband or ex-partner is also part of the system. Their position has to be acknowledged. Conversely, if their positions are not being respected or if the first relationship actually ended in an imbalance, this means that the second relationship/marriage derived a sort of gain from this loss. Because of this, the second marriage will feel a need to compensate the first marriage for their loss, and this dynamic will be especially obvious if the first marriage ended in some form of tragedy. Some of the unconscious ways people might try to compensate for this would be a failure in their marriages, physical or mental problems, failures and losses at work or in their careers, or the child they give birth to might be identify with the previous partner and thus create relationship problems between parent and child, or the child might even end up having a broken marriage, etc (Hellinger, 2001b).

Then, how should we improve the above-mentioned situations?

Firstly, on our own part, we have to be fair when we separate with our partners. If we owe them anything, we have to repay for it; if the knots in our hearts are not unraveled, we will have to find a way to come into reconciliation with them. If it is not possible to meet our previous partners, we can do some good deeds in their names as a form of repayment. Most importantly, even though we are already separated, we will still have to keep a place in our hearts for them and admit that these people are our exes.

Towards our parent's previous partners, we have to respect them. If he or she did not "make room for the later partner", we would not exist; therefore, not only do we have to respect their order and position in our family, we have to do some good deeds on their behalf to remember them. In this way, we will not use intangible losses as a form of compensation. Instead, we can create better things and a better life out of this tragedy. This is the right way bring our affinity with them to a wholesome completion.

Monetary Disputes

In the company, family or interpersonal interaction, the giving and taking of money must be balanced. If improper benefits are obtained because of the loss of balance, then the system will invisibly lose some money or cause some losses to rebalance this imbalance. Sometimes because of the improper gains of the past members, but it may make the whole or later members of the system pay the price. This situation can happen in the company system or the family system (Horn & Brick 2005).

Wei Zheng is a well read and well exposed business consultant and all his siblings are all intelligent management talents. Even though the three siblings often care for each other, but they often quarrel as well. Even though all three of them work very hard but they seem to face many challenges in their careers; and the most interesting thing about them is that they all have the ability to make a lot of money but never seem to be able to keep the money they make.

Wei Zheng, who thinks rather highly of himself, feels that since all three of them have multiple talents, they will definitely be able to help each other resolve their problems and their financial situation will definitely improve. However, a few years down the road, not only did things not get better, the three of them started to communicate less and the situation in their careers and finance seems to be getting from bad to worse. In fact, Wei Zheng had to pay for the workshop in installments in order to take part in it.

I told him, "Systemic Constellations can also be used to explore our relationship with money. Let's explore the relationship between your 'sibling relationship' and 'money'. Perhaps there is a connection between the two."

I placed all three siblings in the constellations, found another participant to represent "money" and included him into the constellations. In the constellations, we saw that the three siblings had their heads facing the floor and they were standing very far apart from each other. Money was standing far away in a corner and no one seems to be concerned about money at all.

"All of you are not concerned about money, no wonder you cannot keep your money."

The three sibling representatives feed backed to us that they seem to "feel a sense of guilt towards money and dare not look at it in the eye."

I asked Wei Zheng, "What is the financial situation of your father?"

"My father is a teacher and has been leading a hard life. He doesn't seem to be getting along well with his siblings as well. I think they got into a dispute over money and stopped contacting each other after that."

"What about your grandfather's generation?"

"I heard that my great grandfather was a very rich man and he had the ability to earn a lot of money. However, my grandfather was considered a wastrel. After he inherited the massive fortune from his father, he wasted all his money away with excessive spending, gambling and donation and he eventually brought about the family's decline.

And so, I added the grandfather and great grandfather into the constellations. The grandfather had his head downcast and was moving backwards but the great grandfather was a powerful figure as he stood there. He was very angry at his son and felt that his son was a weakling. At the same time, the great grandfather was the only person who walked towards the money. He thought that this was his money and wanted to grab hold of it.

But something strange happened. Money was very afraid of the great grandfather and kept avoiding him.

"Do you know how your great grandfather got his money?"

"I am not sure. I think he earned it by building a business."

"Did he have any financial disputes with anyone or received any improper gains from anyone?"

"I heard he was doing business with some foreigners… I am not sure if he sold opium? Maybe he did not have any financial disputes with anyone?"

"It's ok, we will know if we test it out."

I got someone to represent the owner of the money. When I added the person into the constellation, money became very happy and immediately moved close to its owner. But the great grandfather tried to block its way and the three of them got into a tussle.

The more money wanted to go near to its owner, the more the great grandfather wanted to hold on to it. As he grabbed hold of money, he shouted, "This is my money!"

"The truth is out. It is very obvious that there is a problem with this money. There must have been some financial dispute between them and from the response of the money, we can deduce that most of it did not belong to your grandfather. If your grandfather's wealth was mostly accumulated through dishonest means, then the rest of the people in the family who inherit it like your grandfather, father and future generations who have benefitted directly or indirectly from it will have to pay the price. "

"No wonder we all feel guilty whenever we see money. It feels wrong to keep it beside us. So now, what can we do?"

"You have to sincerely repent!"

I guided the great grandfather to say to the person who had at financial dispute with him, "I am sorry, I took your money."

But the great grandfather was unwilling to do that. "There is my money here too!" he grabbed hold of money tightly but money kept wanting to move away sideways.

"This financial dispute is very huge. I guess part of the money belongs to your great grandfather and part of it belongs to the other person but your great grandfather wanted to take all of it."

Both parties were caught in a deadlock for a few minutes, it seems they are unable to come to reconciliation.

I had a sudden inspiration and I got Wei Zheng to kneel down in front of his great grandfather and the person he was having the financial dispute with. First I asked him to say to his grandfather, "My dear great grandfather, thank you, I am your future generation. Thank you for working so hard for this family and earning money for the family. We have gained much from you and we will continue to keep the portion of money belonging to us and let it flourish; as for the part that does not belong to us, I will handle it appropriately. Please do not worry."

Wei Zheng and his siblings made a kow tow to their great grandfather and at this moment, the great grandfather finally loosened his hold on money.

Following that, I got Wei Zheng to kneel down in front of the person who had a financial dispute with his great grandfather and say, "I am sorry, my family took money from you that should not have belonged to us. Now I sincerely apologize to you. I promise I will use this money to do some good deeds for you. Please put your hearts at ease."

The three siblings kow towed to that person and he also loosened his grip on the money.

Now, money can finally stand calmly between their great grandfather and the other party. I invited the great grandfather to pass on the money that belongs to him to their grandfather, their father and finally, the three siblings. "Now that the three of you are gathered together, the money that belongs to your family has also been passed on. You have to work hard to show your respect for your great grandfather; at the same time, you have to use the part that was ill gotten and transform it into charity work, walk out from your guilt and create more love to share with more people.

"I will definitely do that." Wei Zheng nodded his head at me.

Two years later, I heard that Wei Zheng has become more successful in his career. His sales kept increasing and not only did he clear his debts, he also saved up quite a sum of money. His siblings also found new jobs and their bosses admired them and so their careers are also steadily developing.

I send my deepest blessings to them.

Loss As A Result Of Ill Gotten Gains

There is a huge balancing force at work in nature working in the operation of the planets, day and night, man and woman, yin and yang and the desire to balance is one of mankind's innate natures. In the previous chapters, we have learnt the importance of balance between man and woman in a relationship.

In addition, monetary interactions between people have to be in balance as well. If there is a imbalance in the way money is treated or used or if there are ill gotten gains or even if one party feels that there is a balance but the other party thinks otherwise, money disputes will be created and this sort of imbalance might implicate our family members, just like what happened in Wei Zheng's family.

When we say "ill-gotten gains" we are talking about using unfair methods to get benefits and profits. These are considered "improper gains". Regardless of whether it is us receiving improper gains at the expense of other people or other people trying unfairly get any benefits out of us, they are all considered ill-gotten gains. For example, appropriation of property, swindling people of their lands and properties, producing fake goods and even cutting corners when completing a piece of work, etc all fall under this category. When this happens, both parties will get into a dispute. The larger the amount involved, the more unfair it is, the bigger the dispute will be. Why? That is because as a result of the improper gains, the person who is being cheated might make losses, turn bankrupt or even commit suicide and this may affect all their future generations as well. The grievance against the person who had treated them unfairly will be passed on to their future generations and they too will continue to curse on the person through the next generation. That is why when the deceiver gets hold of any ill-gotten gains and pass them on to their future generation, the future generation will definitely pay a price—on the surface, it would seem as if they have benefitted from this ill gotten gain but in actual fact, they may have to pay the price many times over (Horn & Brick 2005).

All thisprinciples that we observed from thousands of Systemic Constellations cases are in actual fact very common in the news or around us. For example, the first generation of some family corporation may have used unlawful or unfair means and earn a lot of profits. By the second generation, they will get into disputes and start to sue each other over money and the siblings will start to quibble and fight over money. These are not uncommon at all. In actual fact, such a situation is not only observable in families or organizations, a few thousand years ago, the Taoist wisdom classic, Book of The Ultra Supreme One's Tractate on Actions and Their Retributions (《太上感應篇》) already states, "People who wrongfully seize the property of others, will see their wives, children and family pay the price and compensate for their sins, even unto death. Those who do not die will meet with disasters of water, fire, theft, loss of goods, disease, slander and more until it offsets their unlawful appropriations. Eventhough that person dies, there still remain unpunished crimes, the bad luck is visited upon the future generations." (諸橫取人財者，乃計其妻子家口以當之，漸至死喪；若不死喪，則有水火盜賊，遺亡器物，疾病口舌諸事，以當妄取之值。死有餘責，乃殃及子孫。) (Huang, 2003).

The root of solving this would be to return to the "Principle of Balance": we can become rich but not at the expense of making other people poor; should we have done anything bad unto others, we have to repent and change. We have to return the ill gotten gain and use their good name to get involve in more charity work as a way of repaying whatever we owe; whatever bad things others have done to us, we have to use a correct method to seek justice or to forgive and forget while learning our lesson from it; we have to remind ourselves to be aware of all our thoughts and emotions, when running our careers, always go for a win-win strategy; treat nature with humility and love to create a balanced and harmonious society. In this way, the Principle of Balance that has been operating from the past to present will give us returns- whatever we do, whatever we get, however we treat others, however others will treat us.

Monetary Principle of Balance: In Addition To A Win-Win Situation, Give A Little More

When running an enterprise, we are always working on achieving our goals and aiming to perpetually grow. Other than not being greedy for "improper gains", if we take this one step further, it is vital that we fervently make good use of the Principle of Balance.

How do we make good use of the Principle of Balance?

We know that when other people receive our "goodness", regardless of whether they are aware, their innate need to balance will kick in. Therefore, they will feel as if they owe us something. And at this moment, if both parties deliver their goods, complete the transaction and no longer owe each other anything, then, this relationship will have ended and we will not know when the next transaction will take place. However, if a fair trade or a win-win situation occurs, we can also choose to give the other party a little more. When we do that, how do you think they will feel? Regardless of whether they are aware, they other party will unconsciously feel that they need to repay us and therefore, when there is good news, they will inform us or they will become interested in other products that we represent or may even refer their friends to buy more of our products, etc, allowing our business to continuously grow and as there will be an endless stream of orders. Many successful entrepreneurs understand this theory and follow it religiously like following the bible. This is not making use of the weakness of mankind to operate our business or to have an expectation that the other party will definitely give us something back in return. It is merely understanding and applying the hidden dynamics of the Monetary Principle of Balance: other than the balance of tangible wealth and assets, there is also a balance in intangible wealth and assets.

Those financial giants who are fraudulent towards their customers such as Lehman Brothers may seem to benefit from a huge sum of money for a short while but they have also created a huge debt of intangible wealth and assets and therefore, they will never be able to keep this money and may even need to pay back their debt many times more. Conversely, many companies or organizations are working hard at their management and bringing in the energy of love and contribution to the work they do. One good example is the famous charity organization, Buddhist Compassion Relief Tzu Chi Foundation. Their total net worth is in fact higher than many of the Fortune 500 companies. Every year, they can chalk up to billions of turnover and have numerous volunteer workers who work there and help out for free simply because they feel a sense of pride to be associated with this organization. Their volunteers include high net worth individuals like entrepreneurs, professors, doctors and many others from the top echelons of the society. Why are they so successful? The founder, Dharma Master Cheng Yen's philosophy was "love for all sentient beings". She once said, "When we give a physical object to others, we are (also) giving ourselves intangible blessings." This sentence is sufficient to explain their huge success: because they make good use of the Principle of Balance (Huang, 2003).

In actual fact, Lao Tzu (l. c. 500 BCE, Author of Tao Te Ching), who is well versed in the principles of nature has long said, "The sage does not accumulate (for himself). The more that he expends for others, the more does he possess of his own; the more that he gives to others, the more does he have himself."
(聖人不積，既以為人己愈有，既以與人己愈多。)

Therefore when we give a little bit more, help others a little bit more, it will bring about a next chance to start a positive cycle and it will help us amass our intangible wealth and assets—This is the secret behind the Monetary Principle of Balance.

Unconscious Conflict- Perpetrator Vs Victim

Sometimes, we are not in the position to interfere with the family secrets within our family system. Any disrespectful prying into the secret is considered offensive. The only way the secret will be friendly to us is when we behave humbly towards it (Dasberg, 2000; Hellinger, 2003a).

Wang Yan, who is sitting beside me, left her hometown to work in Shenzhen. She looks like a strong woman and seems very aggressive. The moment she started talking, she spoke about wanting to understand the current situation of her younger brother and younger sister.

I shared a little story with her, "It is said that one day, the God of Fate has a curtain in front of him and a curious man wanted to secretly open the curtain up to take a peek inside. In the end, he saw a dead man behind the curtain. It was the last man who tried to take a secret peek."

This is a simple and yet thought-provoking story. It tells us about how sometimes the truth can be cruel and at the same time, it is a good reminder for Wang Yan that some things are not what an elder sister should be privy to.

Wang Yan was in deep thought for a while and she nodded her head with understanding. "Yes, this is what I have to learn. Many times, I think I am too much or too over."

"That is very good. When you bring in your respect for your family and for me, you will be able to learn from it."

Once we understand our role and position, we can continue the constellations work and only then can the old stories in our family become clearer.

Wang Yan started sobbing as she shared her story. During the Cultural Revolution, her uncle (mother's sister's husband) reported to the authorities that her maternal grandfather had secretly hidden gold and the grandfather was thus put to death. He was only 50 years old at that time. During the constellations, Wang Yan's younger brother and sister went surprisingly close to the grandfather who was driven to his death. They would like to protect him but Wang Yan was standing closer to the person who had driven her grandfather to his death. Both groups took to their own sides and looked at each other with enmity.

The conflicts of the Cultural Revolution and the unresolved knots in the hearts of the previous generations, through the passing down from generations to generations, has given Wang Yan and her siblings and unconscious burden of experiencing the opposing emotions of the "victimizer" and the "victim". And this conflict is being replayed once again in their sibling relationships with each other.

I told Wang Yan, "Now I understand what is causing the conflict between you and your brother and sister and why you give other people such a strong feeling of aggression."

"No wonder my younger siblings do not like me and are afraid of me for no reason." Wang Yan felt very aggrieved.

And so it seems that within the hatred that was triggered during this great historical era, not only were the victimizers strangers but it also included a family member. How can it be easy to face up to the fate of such great tragedy and the huge price we have to pay...

I tried to get the uncle and the others who had driven the grandfather to death to say, "Sorry," to the grandfather.

However, there was merely silence. It seems like they wanted to apologize but lack the courage to do so.

Both victim and victimizer where deadlocked in their opposition.

Time continued to tick away. This unfortunate tragedy has caused much pain but how do we give it the forgiveness it requires? Not only will the victim require courage, the victimizer will need even more courage just to say that they are sorry.

"He may have driven your grandfather to his death but this was mainly caused by the historical environment of those times. Should they not be born against such historical background, he wouldn't have done something like that. Even though he has to take responsibility for it, you also have to understand that this is a historical event where people had to sometimes act against their will," I reminded and added, "Your grandfather was suffering but weren't those people suffering as well? If he does not pass away in peace, you will all not receive any peace."

Time continued ticking slowly away. The air seemed frozen in the time and space of the past. It was filled with heaviness, sadness and also lots of remorse...

At this moment, I suddenly understood that a very important person needed to be added into the constellations- the aunty. Her husband drove her father to his death. She is stuck in the middle and must be in a lot of pain.

When I added the aunty into the constellations, her deep wailing broke through the silence and stalemate of the situation.
"Wa.... Ooooh..." she was on lying the floor and crying desolately.

This energy brought about some changes to her husband and softened the hearts of the other victimizers. Her husband kneeled down in front of Wang Yan's grandfather and was finally willing to kow tow to him as he cried.

"I am sorry, I am so sorry... as a member of the party, it was my duty; but I apologize to you as a person..."

Wang Yan also started crying and in the midst of all the crying, the other victimizers also made a bow towards the grandfather. At this moment, all the people who had suffered during the Cultural Revolution, be it the victims or the victimizers were all finally able to lie down, take a deep breath and close their eyes in peace.

"Please rest in peace!" Wang Yan was choking as she asked her grandfather to rest in peace.

I invited Wang Yan to say repeat the same thing towards the victimizers who caused her grandfather's death, "Please rest in peace!"

I continued to guide her. "I no longer hate you anymore."

"....," Wang Yan was unwilling to say that. She told them honestly and truthfully, "I still hate you a little."

Yes, it is not easy for a huge wound to return to its original state. But as long has one is willing and sincere, one will slowly recover from the hate and pain, just like Wang Yan's siblings. Right after they apologized to the victimizers and kow tow to them, they were able to stand up peacefully.

"This is a huge challenge in our life. If we want to reconcile, we will have to move beyond the acknowledgement we have for victim vs victimizer. We have to be truly grateful from our hearts and be grateful towards our ancestors for the price they have paid," *I encouraged Wang Yan and everyone else in the room.*

"Also, regardless of whether one is a victim or a victimizer, we should all be in service to our great life." *I respectfully pointed this out.*

Finally, Wang Yan was able to face the victimizers calmly.

"I don't hate you anymore," she released them and also released herself.

With her new found peace and her strength as the eldest sister, Wang Yan hugged her siblings and told them, "I also do not hate you anymore."

With the eradication of hate, in its replacement, will be lots of blessings. I invited everyone to stand up and gave a deep bow to all who have suffered in that huge historical event to show their respect. There was peacefulness and calmness all around. Subtly but surely, the sense of peace and blessings surrounds every single person in the room.

Non-Blood Relations: People Who Are Linked To Our Fates

Other than our blood relations, people who have a special affinity with us but are not blood related to us may also have great influence in our lives as their fates are entwined with ours. Therefore, they also belong to our system. They are most often neglected but are the ones who have the greatest impact on our lives (Hellinger, 2003b).

The "whole system view" is one of the important discoveries made in Systemic Constellations. We are all living within systems and have family systems, societal systems, eco systems, etc. Not only that, every person in the system is not a sole person because the system seems to draw some form of energy that binds and connects everyone together. Everybody who belongs to the system needs to have a place within the system and they will then interconnect and influence each other. Therefore, it is very important for us to understand who is included in our family system.

There is a group of people who make up a very direct, intimate system with us. They include our blood relations and also some non-blood related people. Those blood relations who belong to our system include our children, ourselves, our siblings, parents, parent's siblings (our uncles and aunts), our grandparents (both paternal and maternal) and sometimes, they may include one or two of our great grandparents on both sides. All these people who have the same blood flowing through our veins are people we have important relationships with in our family system.

In addition, another group of non-blood relations who also have important relationships with us are included in our system. They also need our acknowledgement and also need a place in our system. These non-blood relations who have intertwined fates with us mostly fall under three categories:

1. **Giving their place to others:** Because the previous partner left their position, it allows the later partner to come into this family. Therefore, previous partners are also part of our family system. For example, our ex-husbands and ex-wives, our ex-partners and even the ex-partners of our parents and grandparents. Take the father for example. If the father has had a girlfriend in an intimate relationship before marrying the mother, it is their breaking up and leaving her position that allows the mother to be together with the father and to give birth to us. Therefore, she has a big influence over us and also belongs to our system.

2. **Improper Gains:** Disputes over improper gains are often passed on to the future generations as they inherit their parent's wealth. This means that the future generations have to bear the burden of the grievance and guilt of this unfinished business. Therefore, regardless of whether this inheritor has benefitted or been harmed, directly or indirectly, he or she will have to pay the price.

    People who accept improper gains will usually find that their family tends to be distant with each other and that the siblings will often be fighting with each other. They will also suffer from failure in their careers or suffer monetary loss. In more serious cases, they may meet with accidents, fall sick and die. It is just as if they have been cursed.

    The dispute over money and the intent behind it will often link up the two families involved. The larger the sum of money involved, the larger the grievance, the more the collective subconsciousness will create a system within those involved in the dispute; Even the victimized family suffers. They might be feeling unjust and find it difficult to get rid of their feelings of hatred and vengeance and so, their future generations will inherit these emotions and get embroiled into the dispute as well. Therefore, even if we are the party being victimized, it is important that we learn how to better resolve the dispute and achieve balance.

Only when we do that can we release ourselves from the dispute.

3. **Life And Death Entanglements:** This refers to things such as killings, murder or accidents and any life and death incidents related to the victim or perpetrator. For example, dying in a car accident or dying as a result of a serious injury.

Regardless of whether we bring harm onto the other party's family or that they bring harm to our family, all these incidents will connect our systems together as the fates of both families gets entwined together and become a larger system. These are huge entanglements that are created from life and death and thus these people will affect us and our future generations. We will also influence them and their future generations.

Let me share another real life example: One of my clients in China had a grandfather who used to be a landlord. He got into a fight and was relegated to the "five black categories[2]" in Chinese Culture Revolution and eventually died fighting. In the Constellations we saw that the grandfather, the father and the people who fought the grandfather to his death seem to have a lot of hatred and strong antagonism between them. The interesting thing is that the grandfather's future generations also exhibited the emotions of the two opposing parties. One was the fear and anger felt by the victim and the other was the aggression and guilt felt by the perpetrator. Because these were two powerful conflicting energies within the same family, therefore there was a lot of conflict within the family and many instances of emotional splits.

---

[2]　　In Chinese Culture Revolution (1966-1976) ,to be labeled one of the 'five black categories' (黑五类) was to be damned on account of one's class status (landlord, rich farmer, counter-revolutionary, bad influencers an rightist). This label was extended to one's family and descendants.

When these emotions of the victim and perpetrator passed down to the next generation, it will usually result in conflicts, siblings getting into fights and disputes with each other or emotional issues like split personality, schizophrenia and unstable mental states.

Principle of Wholeness: Moving Beyond Victim and Perpetrator

With regards to these life and death entanglements and the victim and perpetrator stories, other than learning that everyone has to be accountable for their own actions, what else can we learn from it?

"Reconciling" is the first step. It is one of the most important homework that many families have to do and is also of the main lessons in many people's lives. But how does "reconciliation" come about? This will require some training to develop our inner selves, training ourselves to see beyond our identification to being a "Victim" and/or a "Perpetrator" and see that everything is in fact moving in service to life. And when that happens, "reconciliation" will be made possible. When we are able to give everyone a place in our hearts and not just see ourselves but see them too and when we see each other's pain and that both parties desire peace, we will create the opportunity to awaken our awareness for life and be aware that we are actually part of the same system. When we move one step closer to take a good look at each other and see that the inherent nature of both parties are actually one and the same, love will start to flow and our society will be able to move toward real harmony—a type of true harmony that begins in our soul (Dasberg, 2000; Hellinger, 2003b).

Hsu (2012) discovered that in the traditional Chinese mindset, the concept of moving beyond victim and perpetrator is called "affinity" (緣分). The meaning of "affinity" refers to a group of people, through some special opportunity, getting to meet and have a shared experience. This opportunity to meet and the type of experience is beyond the control of human beings as it is actually taken care of by the much larger power of life. When we go through this shared experience, should our affinity be made whole, the incident would pass; should our affinity be incomplete and there is no reconciliation in our hearts, then it will continue to exert an influence on us until we complete this affinity. This goes beyond the dichotomy of victim and perpetrator and all of it falls under the larger overall plan of life. We are all part of this overall plan of life. Through affinity, we meet with each other, get to know each other and love each other; or we may meet and feel grievance and hatred towards each other or kill each other. But regardless of what life has planned for us, the important point is that it will allow us to experience and fulfill the affinity by making it whole. When we go through this, we will be able to grow and become more abundant. We will also become wiser and become more loving.

Homework: Completing Your Family Systems Chart

There are many ways to draw the family chart (Lin, et al.,2008), but the uniqueness of the Family Constellation's family chart is that it includes blood relationship and non-blood relationship members. Particular emphasis is placed on those family members who have been excluded or neglected, as well as those in non-blood relationships who will have a significant impact on the family.
Let us understand who are the people who belong to our family system and who are the people we have affinity with.

Step 1, Draw Your Family Systems Chart: Firstly, please take out the chart that we have previously drawn. Then, based on the previously mentioned three points and do your best to collect information about who has given their place to others, who may have had improper gains and who has life and death entanglements with our family members. Include these people and use a dotted/patterned line to link them up with our related family members. These are the people who belong to our same system but are not blood related to us. Now, there are both blood and Non blood related members in the chart, they form the complete family system. (Refer to figure 4)

Step 2, To Reconcile In Our Hearts: This is a very important step. After you are done with the chart, please calm down and take another look at all the non-blood related persons in your chart. Give each of them a place in your heart, move beyond your acknowledgement and judgment towards the roles of victim and perpetrator and give them a bow filled with humility. Every day, take a look at one person and start the process of reconciliation in your heart—admit the truth and thank them for their contribution, return them and yourself to the correct positions and finally, bless that everyone involved will achieve peace.

Step 3, Doing Good Deeds On Their Behalf: When you know that a tragedy has ever happened in your family, please do some good deeds for the people involved. Especially if it is a rather serious or critical incident. Don't only do this for your blood related family members but also do it for those non blood related persons in your system. Only then can we get true reconciliation. Also, you may find out about some of your family stories later and you can always add them in at a later date or you could just do the required in your heart as your attitude is all that matters. Besides, you already know what to do now.

(Refer to Figure 4. Chart of both blood and Non blood related members in a complete family system)

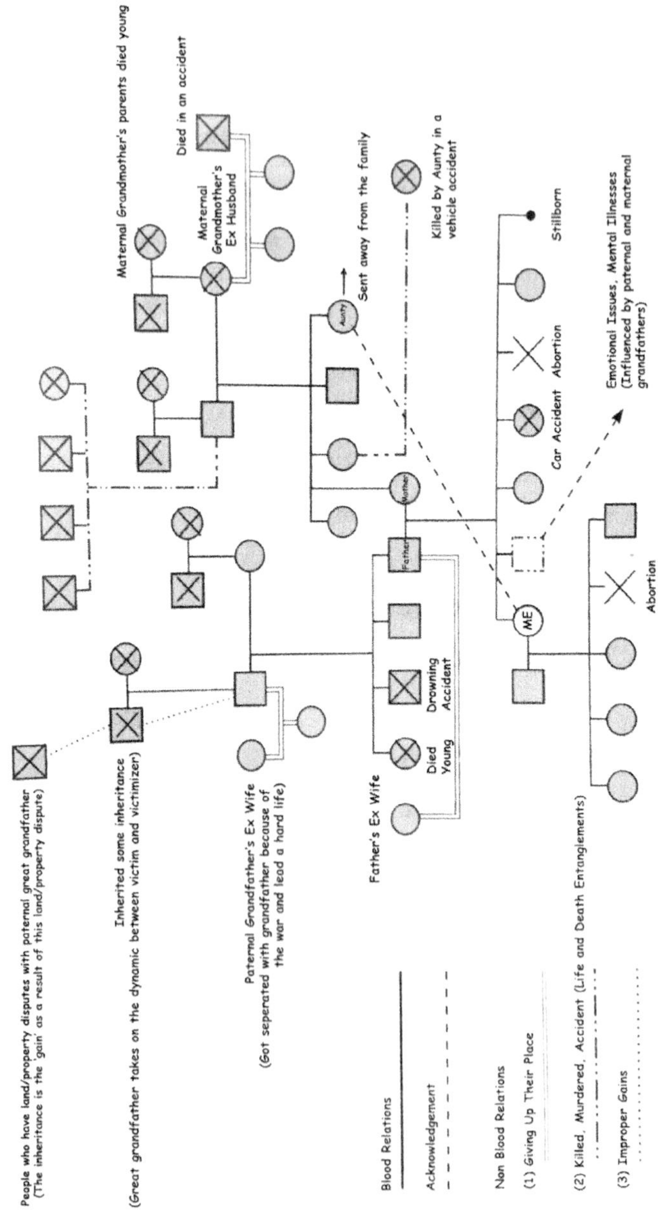
People who have land/property disputes with paternal great grandfather
(The inheritance is the 'gain' as a result of this land/property dispute)
Inherited some inheritance
(Great grandfather takes on the dynamic between victim and victimizer)
Paternal Grandfather's Ex Wife
(Got seperated with grandfather because of the war and lead a hard life)
Father's Ex Wife
Died Young
Drowning Accident
Father
Mother
Aunty
ME
Maternal Grandmother's parents died young
Died in an accident
Maternal Grandmother's Ex Husband
Sent away from the family
Killed by Aunty in a vehicle accident
Car Accident
Abortion
Stillborn
Emotional Issues, Mental Illnesses (Influenced by paternal and maternal grandfathers)
Abortion
Blood Relations
Acknowledgement
Non Blood Relations
(1) Giving Up Their Place
(2) Killed, Murdered, Accident (Life and Death Entanglements)
(3) Improper Gains

Inner Constellation: Harmony Begins in The Soul

This is an Inner Constellation that goes beyond us and our families. It is an exercise that supports historical reconciliation and societal reconciliation. When more people do this from their heart, it will support the soul and hearts of us and our future generations, bringing true peace and the power of a true reconciliation to them.

Let us move upwards
Move upwards
Move upwards a much higher filed
Move upwards to a place where everything is equal
A place where everything has the right to belong
A place where everything is being treated fairly

In that place, we saw that through the history of mankind on earth
Once upon a time, because of the historic events
We had to made some very difficult, painful decisions
We can see how due to the historic battles
Both parties had to be in a fight
Getting in to a conflict with each other, harming each other
Perhaps some of them are our family members
Our elders, our grandfathers and grandmothers
And even some people whom we don't even know their names
Because it was not possible to know their names
Inside this fight, perhaps our family members were persecuted
But they may have also persecuted others
To every single person involved in the persecution, this is a very arduous process
Let us bring in respect and humility
And look at these two groups of people in a fight

Let's give them a deep bow
And say to them,
"Thank you
Because of the price that you paid
We are now able to enjoy our current life of peace and prosperity

Please reconcile with each other
Please rest in peace
The price you paid is not in vain
I will stand on the foundation that you have built
And bring this land and our future generations
A more successful, happy, joyful and harmonious life
Thank you."

Then, look through them and beyond them
Look into far far away to a place that is further beyond them
See the infinitely huge source of life behind them
The source of life shining with infinite golden light
And everything
Regardless of perpetrator or victim
Are all merely in service of this larger life

Under the care of this bigger life
We can see the two groups of people in front of us slowly moving closer together
Slowly moving closer together
We can see them melt into each other and there is no longer a 'you' or a 'me'
Moving beyond their roles as victim or perpetrator
See them turn around together to face this huge source of life
The infinitely huge golden light
Is shining down on them
We can see them merging together with each other
And walking happily towards infinitely huge light
Moving forward
Moving right into this golden light
Returning to the source of life
Merging into this bright golden light filled with blessings
Then, they turn around and sprinkle this golden blessings onto our bodies
We receive these blessings, these love
And put it in our hearts
Once again, we give them a deep bow
And then we slowly come back
To this place

At this moment, our hearts are filled with much more
Much more strength
Much more gratitude
And
Much more love

Chapter 6: Relationship Between Body And Mind

The way a healer understands the root cause and symptoms of sickness, is to view it from a rudimentary level and expand the view gradually to include a broader general view, so that your understanding of the disease can grow from small to big. When you start off from any one point (and follow this method), you will be able to understand all diseases and their harmful effects. It is easy and helpful to talk about the roots and the symptoms of disease. If we look into both the roots and symptoms, we will be able to fine tune the flow of our 'qi' (vital energy of life). Once you understand this, you can overcome all its complexities. This is applicable to all people and it is heaven's will that we do that.

夫標本之道要而博，小而大，可以言一而知百病之害，言標與本，易而無損，察本與標，氣可令調，明知勝複，為萬民式，天之道畢矣。

- **The Huang Di Nei Jing ·Su Wen**/《黃帝內經.素問》

Connections of Mental, Physical And Family:
A Whole System View

Is our relationship with our mind and body good? Do we understand what our mind and body are trying to tell us? Do we know what are the hidden messages behind the emotions that we feel?

Modern medical science has already acknowledged that the body and our hearts and minds are actually an integrated whole and they are tightly linked and connected together. However, we often think that human beings are independent individuals and that our minds and our bodies are independent of each other. If we isolate these parts of ourselves, that might seem to be the case, but we are only half correct. Through thousands and millions of observations made in Systemic Constellations, we have discovered that everybody's mental and physical condition is closely related to the system that they belong to (Hellinger, 2003d). For example, our genes are genetically inherited from our family and our emotions have been influenced by our mothers since we were fetuses. Our characters and our values and beliefs are also shaped through subtle influences by our families. And even when we are fully grown up, all these things still exert and influence on us. These are in fact the influences that our system has on us. Furthermore, this influence also includes a hidden family fate that is unconsciously tied to our fates. Therefore, a person's physical and emotional condition is very much linked to the system that they belong to. And this "whole system outlook" is not only mentioned in psychology, biology and ecology. Even traditional Chinese medicine talks about this (Zhang & Hu, 2018).

The Huang Di Nei Ning ·Su Wen (An ancient Chinese medical text that has been treated as the fundamental doctrinal source for traditional Chinese medicine.) talks about the concepts of "oneness of body and spirit"（形神一體）, "interrelationship between life and nature"（生氣通天）and "synchronicity between man and the universe" （人與天地相參）. It believes not just that a human body is a complete whole but also that the human being is one whole together with the system it belongs to. Therefore, there is a need to understand mankind's physical, psychological and pathological processes through observing the connection between man and their families, societal relations, nature and environment. At the same time, according to the Chinese acupuncture's "Holographic Principle"（全息律）, research proves that all the different parts of the whole system a inter related. Therefore, from a small part of the body, we can understand the whole body (Zhang & Hu, 2018).

This phenomenon of a holographic system (where each piece of the system contains information about the whole system) does not only exist in our human bodies but also exists in the organizations and systems that are made up of human beings. Because we are a part of our family system, our body and mind become the receptor of all related information in the system and we will receive all the collective information in the collective consciousness of the family system. For example, our body may inherit a hereditary disease, our minds may be receiving deep messages about the relationships between family members and the mind and the body will also influence and interchange with each other and therefore, these information would be reflected in our physical conditions and our emotional state. Based on this, we can see that many unexplainable mental and physical conditions are often not a direct result of an issue with one's mental or physical health but actually stems from problems in our systems (Zhang & Hu, 2018). Therefore, I feel strongly that medical science is certain to move towards this whole system view of helping people in the near future. If we can combine both eastern and western medical school of thoughts, psychology and also Systemic Constellations, I believe this will greatly benefit our health and growth.

Love Flowing, Heart Pumping- Heart Attack

Zhang, Ge & Yang (Zhang et al., 2006) investigated the influence of effects on cardiovascular and cerebrovascular diseases. They chose 212 patients to investigate couples' character, economical domination, sexual life, affects, talking with children and the children's filial piety to them. They found that the influences of couples affects and sexual harmony are important to their health, and the influence of children's filial piety to parents is also significant. Let me express it in a simpler an poetic way, that is when our love is able to flow, our heart will bring this love along with our blood and flow throughout our whole body. The following is one of my cases.

Guo An who is 63 this year came to the workshop together with his sister, Jia Mei. Jia Mei had previously attended a series of my trainings and understands Systemic Constellations extremely well. She has been applying all Principles of Relationships in her life and has been sharing them with her family members. After listening to his sister's sharing and encouragement, Guo An developed an awareness that he has been actually shouldering many of the family's dark, heavy fates. Just not so long ago, he was suddenly hit by a case of heart attack. Thankfully, he was resuscitated in time in the hospital. After such a huge calamity where he was given a second chance in life, Guo An lost his gratitude towards life and also started feeling lots of unexplainable fear.

As his father passed away at age 69 due to a heart attack, Guo An was very afraid that he would follow his father's footsteps and that he would be suddenly hit by death without warning, losing even the chance to give his final instructions about any possible arrangements after his death. He was afraid he might just close his eyes and pass away suddenly in agony.

"I have a constant ache in my heart and often feel nausea. Even as I speak, I am feeling a little nauseous," said Guo An.

Jia Mei added, "My brother has often given too much to the family. He is the eldest son and not only does he face the pressure from the elders, he also has to burden the responsibility of taking care of the siblings. Until now, he is still single as he is taking care of my schizophrenic younger brother. Even the friends around him will constantly borrow money from him and fail to return it. Over the years, he has made heavy losses."

I asked them, "What is the function of our heart? It is to deliver blood to our body and also to deliver "love" to our spirit, so that we can receive and give out love. If the delivery of love is blocked, our heart will also develop a blockage. The way to resolve this is to clear up our pipeline of love so that our love and flow around easily and successfully."

I invited someone to represent Guo An and another person to represent his heart. During the process of the constellations, the person who was representing Guo An looked so tired and had such a heavy burden that he collapsed on the floor; and at that point, the person representing his heart also collapsed suddenly on the floor. I got another person to represent Guo An's father and the moment he was added into the constellations, he collapsed onto the floor as well.

There seemed to be some secret we have yet to unravel.

"Did anyone in your family die suddenly?" I asked.

"We are not too sure," said the two siblings, staring in shock at the people who were all collapsed on the ground.

"Was anyone in your family involved in any incident of grievous harm or murder? From the representative's reactions and what you have shared so far, it seems that you are compensating for something. Perhaps, there are some secrets hidden in this family."

The two of them were still unable to remember or come up with anything.

"Good."

I added in another two representatives. One person represented the person in the family who was trying to compensate for something and the other represented this person whom he wants to compensate to. The person who was trying to compensate the other was shivering. He has the posture of a perpetrator. He put his hand over his heart and had the other hand outstretched towards the other person who is being compensated to (who was lying on the floor). It seems as if he had the desire to die in the other person's place. Lying on the floor, the victim clenched his heart and rolled around violently on the floor while wailing loudly.

It is obvious that there is some secret hidden in this family. And these two people definitely hope to rest in peace. When we do not disturb them and look at them with respect, and when we can see them, we open a window of possibility for them to rest in peace.

After a while, without any interruptions or interference by anyone, the perpetrator walked very slowly towards the victim, his hands trembling and tears flowing freely from his eyes. Finally, when both victim and perpetrator clasped on to each other's hands and placed it in front of their hearts, the intense emotions were finally and gradually giving way to peace.

I told Guo An, "Now, you can see that you have been trying to take over their unhappiness. Your father and our brother are doing the same as well. All of you are trying to compensate for something but the way you do us is to unconsciously let yourselves suffer. You have been repeating the tragedy as a show of your loyalty to your family. Sadly, this sort of compensation is not helpful for the other party at all and will even allow the unhappiness to go on. Therefore, you have to change the way you show love."

Guo An stood up. He went over to where the two of them are and kneeled down before them to give a kow tow. He touched his heart and touched their hearts and said, "Even though I do not know the details of what happened, but I respect what has happened to you. In the following days, my heart will continue to pump for you, and I will do some good things in your memory."

I asked Guo An to touched the other party and allow all the love and sadness to flow through his hands from his heart to the two people. Now that the love is moving in a flow, it is no longer on standstill, the two people (one who needed to be compensated and the other who is compensating for something) were finally able to close their eyes and rest in peace. Both parties are reconciled and no longer separated. In the end, I also included the schizophrenic brother into the constellations. I got the brother to kneel down facing the two parties and touch them so that he can integrate their strength into his heart. After a while, the brother's representative started to loosen up and looked visibly more relaxed.

The whole constellations ended peacefully.

When Guo An went into his seat, he shared that he felt that his heart is much more relaxed now.

Inspired, I told Guo An and his sister, "This could be an incident where two members of the family harmed each other or it could be an accident which resulted in a death. But what happened in your family is a real miracle. The two parties involved can just reconcile so easily. This means that they have both been waiting for this reconciliation to happen. And you're having a sudden heart attack and being resuscitated after that is also a miracle. I hope that the both of you will treasure these miracles and use a better way to share the joy of life.

Guo An and his sister nodded their heads.

Not long after, Jia Mei wrote me a letter:
Since I started learning about Family Constellations, I have been readjusting myself so as to let go of the heaviness in my heart and I have been indirectly trying to help my family. I am really happy. When I accompanied my brother to the workshop, I was quite worried that the underlying dynamic will be so powerful it will overwhelm us but perhaps like what you have said, there are a lot of miracles helping us. After the constellations, both me and my brother felt very relaxed. This is an experience we have never experienced before. At home, I can finally experience the flow of love between the family members. In

addition, I believe that when I move in a positive direction and live my life to the fullest, it means that I am honoring the innocent people who died. And this is the best direction that love can flow towards. I will continue to move towards this goal as I continue my life. Thank you very much, Teacher."

Principle Of Flow: Transform The Attitude Of Compensation

Our physical symptoms and mental conditions are a type of message, they reflect the imbalance that is happening in our system and show us if there are "unfinished business" or "excluded members" in our system. The group of organs in charge of our physiological function will bring certain things to our awareness by becoming sick. This may not be a bad thing at all. For example, the heart is the main organ in charge of the delivery of nutrients and spiritually, it is also the entrance and exit for love to flow in and out. From the above-mentioned real-life example about the dynamics of systems, we saw that Guo An and his father's sudden acute heart problems is not just a reflection of their hereditary health issues from the family but also a reflection of the fact love has stopped flowing within the system. Through Systemic Constellations, we are able to show that the source of this issue is that they were trying to compensate for a family secret which involved some sudden tragedy. The perpetrator often longs to compensate and the victim often longs to be seen. Even if the client himself has not much information about what may have happened in the past, we will still be able to find a solution (Ulsamer, 2005).

And what is the solution?

From my experience of helping thousands of cases, it isn't unconsciously using monetary losses or a physical illness to compensate them but rather, to show respect for the two unfortunate parties by doing some good in their loving memory. In this way, we can transform the unconscious compensation into more happiness and success. We can even share this happiness and success with them as this love that is filled with awareness can now flow through our hearts. This is the best way we can pay tribute to the victim and perpetrator and return them their dignity.

Inner Constellation: Listening To Messages From Your Body

Any physical condition or disease is actually a message from our body. It tells us:
- which part of our body we haven't been taking care of;
- which part of our thoughts or our emotions have been in imbalance;
- who are the people we have not let go of or have not accepted;
- what are the unfinished businesses in the family;
- who are the ones we have been disrespectful to;
- who are the people who have been excluded or forgotten by us.

Therefore, let us listen closely to these messages and see them in a whole new light as we try to understand what our body is trying to tell us. This is a very good Inner Constellation exercise. You may choose to read out slowly or get a friend to help guide you along:

Please let your heart become calm and quiet
Sit down or lie down in a position that allows you to concentrate
Connect with and take a moment to feel your body
Put your hands on the place of your disease or its symptoms
Imagine that you are going into your body
Go right into the tissues of that particular organ
Connect with and feel those tissues from within
Take a look at this symptom
Open your heart
And wait
Wait for the message that this symptom is trying to pass to you

When you take a deeper look at this symptom
What people do you see
Who do you see

Give them a good look
And tell him or her
"I can see you now
I can see you now
I respect your fate
I will give you a place in my heart again
I can see you now"

Now we wait
Open your heart and wait
What message is this symptom trying to tell you
It may be a simple sentence
It may be one or two words
When it appears
This message becomes a precious gift
Keep this precious gift in your heart
It could be a gift filled with healing powers
A gift filled with blessings
For you
And your family
A gift it is

I Want To Go Home- Depression And Panic Attacks

More and more psychologists have applied the family system theory and treatment and have achieved positive results (Nichols & Schwartz, 2001; Franke, 2003b; Cohen, 2006; Essl, 2006). From my experience in psychotherapy for patients in psychiatric hospitals, it is important for the family to sort out the entanglements behind the family system when everyone in the family can return to their rightful positions and take up their own responsibilities, the family will no longer be impeded by entanglements. It would rather become a strong helping force among every member of it. The following is also a case of mine.

Cai Xia is a 50-year-old teacher in China. I met her when I was working as a therapist in the mental faculty ward of Shi Li Hospital. Prior to this, she had been seeing doctors in the psychiatric department for some time. However, in recent weeks, her emotions have been very unstable and she has been suffering from serious depression and panic attacks. Therefore, her doctors arranged for her to be awarded.

After staying in the hospital for about a month, her depression got worse. Her face was pale and her expression dull. She seemed totally disinterested in any activities held in the ward. She refused to take part in any activity and what is even stranger is that she would sometimes lie down on the bed and feel a heavy weight press down on her chest. Her whole body will turn rigid and she will have difficulty breathing. She will start to feel panicky and shiver and sometimes, she even breaks out in cold sweat. As there did not seem to be any improvement in her case, her doctors were hoping that she can undergo psychological therapy to supplement what they are already doing and thus, they arranged for her to see me.

I would talk with her once a week. During the course of her therapy, I tried to find out more a out her family.

"My father and mother are very good to me. After I got married, my husband was also very good to me." Cai Xia answered.

"Why are you admitted to hospital now?" I asked her.

"I don't know. When I was at home, I often felt depressed and would spend the whole day staring into space. I didn't feel like doing anything. Some time ago, for some unknown reason, I started to carry my bag and walk around in my house while shouting, "I want to go home! I want to go home!""

"That is indeed very strange." I said.

"Yes, it is! My husband asked me, "This is your home. Where else do you want to go? Or do you mean you want to go back to your parent's house?" But I didn't know why I was doing this. I just continued to carry my bag and walk around in my house while shouting, "I want to go home! I want to go home!" eventually, it got very serious and my husband had no choice but to send me to hospital."

"This is indeed very strange. Let us explore this together."

I used Systemic Constellations to evaluate this unexplainable emotion. During the constellations, Cai Xia was all huddled up and shivering in a corner. I asked Cai Xia if anyone in her family had been grievously harmed or murdered and she suddenly thought of her paternal aunt."

"My aunt committed suicide."

"Why did she do that?"

"When my aunt was very young, she was fostered out to another family. Her foster parents were very strict with her and they often beat her up. One time, the weather was very chilly and she didn't have a blanket. So she took a new blanket in the house to cover herself up. When her foster father found out, he said how could she use this new blanket and gave her a sound beating. The next day, my aunt committed suicide by hanging herself."

At this moment, I made a connection: Perhaps at that moment, Cai Xia's aunt only had one thought in mind-- "I want to go home"!

Cai Xia continued, "It is very strange, we rarely talk about this incident. It is as if everyone had forgotten this aunt. But once, while I was teaching, I shared this story with my class, the story of someone committing suicide over a blanket..."

"Good, let's add your aunt into the constellations."

When the aunt was added into the constellations, the person representing Cai Xia voluntarily moved closer to the aunt. Finally, she squat down beside her aunt and started shivering violently. This image depicts how close Cai Xia is to her aunt. It seemed as if she felt some sort of unexplainable connection and identified strongly with her aunt and that is why she undertook the emotions of her aunt. Cai Xia was shriveled up in a corner and shivering badly, I guess this could be the exact same behaviour her aunt had when she was being beaten.

The truth has finally come to light, the next step is to find a solution. Therefore, I invited Cai Xia to personally mourn for her aunt.

Cai Xia kneeled down beside the representative who represented her aunt and hugged her tightly. As tears gushed out of her eyes, she said, "My dear aunt, a tragedy has befallen you. You must have felt so sad and must have wanted very much to go home. But everyone had forgotten about you. I am so sorry…"

I guided Cai Xia to continue on, "Aunt, you must be feeling very lonely and want very much to go home. I can understand your feeling and now, I can see you again. I will let our family members remember you and we will put you in our hearts and bring you home."

Cai Xia hugged her aunt silently.

After a few minutes, I could feel that the previous fear and sadness in the air dissolve and in replacement, was a deep sense of peace and serenity.

Moved deeply, the aunt's representative finally closed her eyes. Cai Xia wiped off her tears and made a bow to her aunt.

"Dear aunt, I will do some good deeds in your memory. Please rest in peace!"

Cao Xia made another deep bow to her aunt.

When we have completed the constellations, I asked Cai Xia, "How do you feel now?"

Cai Xia answered serenely, "I feel very, very relaxed."

Since the constellations, Cai Xia has made a remarkable transformation. The nurses noticed that she started to smile more. Her cheeks also became rosier and she started to take part in the events in her ward actively. From our weekly conversations, I can see her improvement. She says that her panic attacks have improved tremendously, her chest no longer feels heavy and she feels more energetic too.

After three months in the hospital, she was finally ready to go home. Our therapy sessions were also decreased to once every two weeks for the next three months. Cai Xia worked hard at her recovery. She started to exercise and took part in some gatherings. When her husband accompanied her to her sessions, he also mentioned that she has made great improvements. Not only did all her strange behaviour disappear, the whole family even went tour together a few days ago!

Principle Of Wholeness: Re-acknowledging The "People Who Were Excluded"

The "Principle of Wholeness" states: Regardless of their behaviour and what happens to them, as long as one belongs to this family system, they will have a right to belong to this system and will forever have a place within the system. However, whenever someone who belongs to our family system gets "excluded" for certain reasons, it will create a black hole within the system and hence the entanglements (Hellinger, 2001a).

From my experiences, usually, there are a few reasons why people become "excluded":

Number 1, a sad tragedy may have befallen one of the family members (for example, accidents, suicides and chronic illnesses) and because we cannot accept what has happened to them, we may consciously or unconsciously forget them.

Number 2, one of the family members may have done something bad (for example, seizing other people's money, incest, violence, making false accusations and/or committing crime) and because we cannot accept what they have done, we exclude this person secretly in our hearts; this person then has no status within the family and everyone will not acknowledge him or her as part of the family.

Number 3, some of our family members were fostered out since young or may have even died at a young age. They too have a right to belong to this family but we often tend to neglect or forget them. This is also a form of exclusion.

In this example, Cai Xia's aunt was being fostered out and had committed suicide. Regardless of whether her family had been conscious or unconscious about it, she was in fact being excluded and forgotten. When the system contains someone who is being excluded, the future generations will try to fill up this black hole in the system, just as Cai Xia did; when she tried to take over her aunt's position in the family, she had unconsciously taken on all her aunt's feelings and therefore suffered from all sorts of unexplainable emotions like depression, anxiety and fear. However, once her aunt's position had been reaccepted, re-acknowledged and seen and once her aunt is given a place in the hearts of the family members, Cai Xia will no longer need to take the place of her aunt in the family. When she returns her aunt's position to her, she can move back to her rightful position in the family. When we return the position back to the person who is being excluded, "filling up" and "entanglement" will thus be cut off. We become separated from the person and thus these feelings we have taken over will disappear as well (Hellinger, 2001a).

So what does it mean to "undertake feelings?" How are these undertaken emotions different from other emotions?

Undertaking Feelings

"Undertaken feelings" are not just an important discovery in the area of Systemic Constellations, it has also made a huge contribution in the application of modern psychology (Cohen, 2006; Hellinger et al.,1998).

First of all, we should understand about "feelings". Based on Hellinger's categorization, supplemented by my experience in psychology work, feelings can be basically categorized under 4 categories (Hellinger, 2001a):

1. Primary feeling: It is a human instinct emotional reaction. When Something bad happens, we get angry; when we encounter sad things, we will be sad; our emotion disappeared after those incidents.

2. Secondary feeling: For example: when we encounter a certain thing, our primary feeling should be angry, but by feeling helpless instead. This helpless feeling is the secondary feeling, or when a member of our family pass away, we should feel sad, but in anger, complaint or alienation instead of sadness. This is another example of explanation for the **phenomenon** of secondary feeling. This is also a psychological mechanism mentioned by Freud in his psychoanalysis.

3. Undertaking feeling: this kind of emotion is hard to be self-aware. When the undertaken emotions come out in one's mind, it is so unexplainable to everyone sometimes. From the observations of Systemic Constellation, we did find that people undertake emotion from others.

From my experiences, I found that undertaking feeling mostly fall under three common types:

Number 1, undertaking the parent's feelings by the child. For example, if the father is very angry towards the mother, the child will undertake his father's emotions; or if the mother wishes to leave the family, the child will undertake this feeling and develop a desire to leave the house or family too. One possibility is that they will develop a wish inside their deep heart, "Mum, I will go with you," sort of thinking and if the mum had chosen to leave the family by dying, the emotion and thinking that the child has undertaken will then be, "Mum, I will go with you into death," or sometimes, it may even be a case of, "Mum, I will die for you." I have seen and observed these unconscious thoughts in many unfortunate cases and this type of unconscious thinking is often very difficult to detect. However, we will be able to see it clearly through Systemic Constellations.

Number 2, undertaking the feelings of some relatives we have never met before. This sort of undertaking happens even more deeply within our soul. An example would be to undertake our grandfather, grandmother or great grandparent's emotions. This happens even if we have not ever lived together with them before, or may not have even met them before. For example, the grandfather might have left his hometown and because his heart is filled with a longing for his hometown, he will desire a sense of belonging that he lacks. And the future generations will thus develop a strong desire to belong for no reason.

Number 3, undertaking the unfinished businesses in the family system. This is especially so if the people in the same family system go through a huge trauma together. For example, someone of the family may be murdered or killed by other family members, and this sort of huge conflict and sense of unease will permeate the whole family system. If the generation who experiences that does not come to a reconciliation, these feelings of separation will flare up in the next generation. Sometimes, it may even cause schizophrenia or other atavistic mental illnesses. This is because there exist two strong emotions of "being victimized" and "being perpetrator" within the family. Therefore, the family will undertake on this feeling of splitting and unease. However, as everyone undertakes the emotion to a different extent, they may express it differently. I believe that many of you may have been aware of the existence of such strange cases where the whole family seems to share some similar but strange emotions.

4. Meta feeling: it is a hyperphysical feeling, the feeling of emptiness. When we connect with the power of now; stand in the position right belongs to us; focus and calm, we will be bathed in boundless, and awareness. The meta feeling leads us to look after all those happenings in our life with a gem-pure self awareness. Under this circumstance, we can love or help and even take any actions by showing a great mercy rather than just love in desire. This is a more powerful way to love. For those who are interested in helping, the abilities of focus and being centred are crucial.

Therefore, in the world of psychology, the Undertaken feelings are an very important discovery. It is especially helpful in providing assistance to people in therapy. It helps us to look at a human being from a different point of view, a view that is even more all-encompassing, a view that allows us to see how a system can actually affect the emotions and behaviour of a person and how we face up to the events that have taken place within our family system?
At the same time, I feel that this has great impact on the application of Post-modern psychology.

Postmodern psychotherapy has started to view individuals in context of the life they have had in order to understand them. Add in the experiences we have gained from Systemic Constellations and we can expand this context to include one's family system. In some cases, we may even expand the context further to include one's national and cultural context into the system. This will allow us to see how the people who are being excluded in the system will affect a person and even how people may sometimes undertake feelings stemming from their family history or historical incidents. Therefore, this holistic view towards psychotherapy will certainly be an important trend in future and will become one of the prerequisites of all therapists should have knowledge of. This will help us to better understand our clients and patients and allow us to better contribute to the happiness and well-being of them and their families (Walsh, 2005; Cohen, 2006; Nelles, 2006).

One Tragedy Is Enough- Suicide and Rebirth

Family system theory has also been used in psychological grief counseling. Research has found that using family system treatment perspectives can improve the relationship between the client and the family, reduce the risk of depression and suicide, and enhance the client's strength in dealing with unfortunate events (Franke, 2003b; Tien, 2020). When we face the death of a loved one by suicide, feeling sad does not mean that we will collapse. Some people may cry loudly but still feel strong within their hearts...

Jie Li is still grieving over the loss of her husband. Her husband had chosen to hang himself when his wife and daughter had gone over to China to bring him back to Taiwan.

Suppressing all her pain and withholding her emotions, Jie Li was most concerned with how this might affect her children. In the process, she had forgotten to take good care of herself and because she had been suppressing all these massive emotions, she had often the thought of committing suicide.

Biting her teeth, Jie Lie told us, "If not for our children, I would have followed him a long time ago."

"If you were to do that, what would your husband think? What would become of your children?"

She hung her head down and kept quiet.

I asked my assistants to help to represent her husband, her 8-year-old son and 12 year old daughter and place them in a constellations. The constellations depicted the deeper influences that the death of her husband had on the rest of the family: Jie Li was suppressing all her sadness; her son kept moving backwards so that he could be far away from his family and far away from the other family members. Even though he turned around to look at his mother, he soon had his back facing them again. Her daughter continued to stand by her mother's side to accompany Jie Li.

The pain of losing a loved one permeates throughout the whole family. Her husband was also trying to suppress his emotions and it seemed that he couldn't bear to leave. He stubbornly stood there and refused to lie down in peace. At this moment, his wife started to cry but it sounded like a stifled cry. It was obvious that she was trying hard to suppress her emotions.

I continued to encourage Jie Li, "Try to look at your husband. You can let it out, it is ok."

Jie Li's lips were quivering, her words seem to have gotten stuck at the tip of her tongue and she was unable to express them.

I guided her and helped her expressed her emotions by saying loudly, "Why did you do that?"

"Why did you do that?" After Jie Li said that, she started to cry out loud.

"Louder, why did you do that!" I continued to guide her along.

"Why did you do that!" Jie Li was howling by now.

After she finished, she laid down on the floor and started crying. On the other hand, her son who had overheard his mother's sobs started to cry as well.

Jie Li closed her eyes and laid down on the floor and cried. She continued crying for a few minutes while she lay limply on the floor.

I listened carefully to her cries. Her crying was a release of the pent-up emotions she had. However, it was more of a disappointing sadness rather than her grieve over losing her husband.

I told her, "You have to look at your husband and stop crying with your eyes closed. If you love him, you will be able to look at him and drop down tears of grief."

Jie Li continued to lie limply on the ground. But she managed to open her eyes and look at her husband. I continued to encourage her. "Being sad does not mean that we will collapse. Some people may cry loudly but still feel strong within their hearts."

And indeed, feeling sad doesn't mean we will collapse. Only when we are done with the crying, will we have a chance to learn to wipe away our tears and continue on with our lives.

On the other hand, her husband's representative continued to stand there stubbornly. It seems as if he was unable to rest in peace. I told Jie Li, "This is indeed a great tragedy and a huge cause to feel sad. But even in your sadness, you have to stand up strongly and face your husband truthfully. Now, try to walk slowly towards him and accept his death. Then help him to lie down. This is the last thing you could help him with- to let him rest in peace after death."

Accepting the death of a loved one is indeed difficult for the people who are surviving. Even though Jie Li heard me and was willing to move forward, her movement seemed strained and seemed to take lots of effort.

"Slowly... slowly..." I continued to encourage her.

She sat down on the floor and used her hands to support her body as she climbed towards her husband. She tried very, hard to climb over and tears kept flowing nonstop. She tried to give herself more leverage by standing up but it was still very difficult for her to move forward. In the end, she had to crawl on her fours to move towards her husband.

Just when she finally touched her husband, her son started to move as well. He started to turn to look at his parents. When the father passed away, only when the mother, who is at the front line of the tragedy, is willing to express her grieve, will the children given the permission to grief as well.

Jie Li stood up slowly with the help and support of her husband.

I told Jie Li, "Hug your husband. Hug him and hug him with all your power."

Jie Li hugged her husband tightly and cried loudly.

"I will bring you home… I will bring you home…" she said as she tried to help her husband lie down. But her husband refused to lie down. He wanted to get closer to his children, his 8- and 12-year-old son and daughter.

The love of the dead is a love filled with a reluctance to let go. Likewise, are those who are alive not filled with this reluctance as well?

When Jie Li promised to continue living her life well and take good care of her children, the husband who had been suppressing his emotions started to cry. The emotions in this family are finally moving in a flow—their love is finally starting to flow.

Yes, when a tragedy happens, once is already enough.

Just like how the representative of the 8-year-old shared, "I don't like this to happen to my father but my mother's emotions are also very important to me. When my mother could stand up, I felt I became more powerful as well."

Finally, Jie Li told her children, "He will forever be your father. Even though his physical body has left us, he will live forever in our hearts."

Next, she hugged her daughter and her daughter who had all along been just silently looking at her father started crying as well. Finally, everyone was able to express their emotions and they were all huddled together.

Yes, true grief is deep and filled with power.

After some time, the sounds of their sobbing gave way to peace and they started to calm down. The family of four hugged closely together.

By then, the husband was finally able to lie down and rest in peace.

After the constellations ended, I told Jie Li, "When you go home, hug your children more. When children are faced with such sudden events in their lives, the emotions will be accumulated in their body. Hugging them will be very helpful for them. Even if they do not cry out loud, through hugging, they will be able to allow their life energy to start flowing once again.

I added, "Remember to tell them, "Mummy will live on well!" when you hug them."

Jie Li agreed with a smile.

I asked her, "What flower does your husband like?"

"His favourite are lilies."

"This coming Qing Ming Festival (a Chinese festival where the descendents celebrate and honour their ancestors by cleaning up their tombstones and holding a gathering afterwards), bring your children to their father's tomb. Grow his favourite lilies around his tomb and transform your sadness and grief into love. How do you think your husband would feel?"

"Yes, he will be very happy. I will definitely do that." Jie Li smiled as she nodded her head. Her smile expressing a flicker of hope.

One year later, I received a letter: Dear Teacher Chou, I am Jie Li, I do not know if you still remember me. I am the wife who had a husband who hanged himself to death. Today, I brought my children to their father's tomb and we planted a row of lily bulbs around his tomb. The next year, I am certain we will be certain to be greeted with a sea of flowers. We have slowly walked out of the shadow of this incident and are getting better and better. Thank you so much for your help!

When I read the letter, this image invariable came to mind: a sea of lilies gently swaying as the gentle wind blew past and Jie Li and her husband are smiling happily....

Principle Of Flow: Living On Happily

When we open our hearts towards the death of our loved ones, we will truly be able to accept their passing and be able to perceive and feel the love hidden behind the grief— a love that comes from the deceased which is the motivating power that will allow the living to go on living happily. Living happily is also the biggest form of love and respect we can show towards the deceased. This is the Principle of Flow working in our lives. It allows love to flow on to the next generation, flowing on continuously. In future, when it is our time to pass on, wouldn't we also wish for our descendants to live on happily?

Therefore, one tragedy is already enough.

When a tragedy happens, it's purpose is not to tell us how deep the hurt will be but rather, to remind us not to let it unconsciously happen again; the purpose of sad stories that make us weep is not to let us experience deep pain or teach us how to be angry, sad or bitter. Rather it is to awaken our wisdom of love, so that we can learn the lessons that life has for us and not to be unconsciously hurt or be in pain.

Transforming tragedy to power, transforming anger to love and transforming destruction to creation—this is the wisdom of love.

My dears, the road to personal growth and healing is not easy. But if you wish to feel supported along this path, it is actually not that difficult at all. Just like these life examples, we can see and understand that the best support is the love that everyone has for the people around them, it is the love for their ancestors and the love for their descendants. Through tragedies, life teaches us how to love more maturely, through its comedies, life inspires us to feel gratitude and be creative. Therefore, our family stories will no longer stay tragedies and will no longer be filled with entanglements. Instead, they become stories about how generations of love are being passed on from each other.

Individual Constellations: Respect Your Family History And Move Towards A Brighter Future

We are who we are now because of our past. As our families make up our past, we have to understand that we are not trying to search for the root cause of our current issues in the past of our families. Rather, we are trying to respect and learn the lessons that life has given us and our families. If a person carries the notion that it is possible to cut off all ties with their family histories and lead their own lives, it will mean that they are cutting off their roots and putting all the past experience, wisdom and price paid by our ancestors to waste. In actual fact, the more a family has gone through huge upheavals in their fates, the stronger the power of the future generations. Therefore, it is important that we pay gratitude to our family histories with humility and respect and ensure its continuity. Only then can we transform this power to a bigger force and create a better future for both ourselves and our future generations.

The following is a very wonderful constellations exercise. You need to do this with 2 other partners. Please ask one partner to represent your bigger family and place him about 2 meters away in front you. Get the other person to represent your future and place him 2 meters behind you. Afterward, face the two representatives with respect and follow the following guided exercise.

First, face the representative of your bigger family.

With humility
Look at your family
They are the thousands of ancestors from your family
Now, they are like a giant standing right in front of you
They have faced countless difficult challenges and cycles of life and death
However, they remained strong and continued to pass life on
Passing life to your parents
Passing life to you
Their blood is flowing in your body
Without them, you wouldn't exist

Just like you would show gratitude to someone who has granted you life
Show your respect and gratitude
And make a deep bow to the fate of your family
The deeper the better
The deeper the better
Just like how the river of life will flow to the lowest valleys
Your humility will welcome unlimited blessings from your family
Because
Right behind your family
Is an unlimited life
A source of unlimited life

If you feel like kneeling down, you may do so
Use your own way to express your respect and gratitude
Open yourself up
The humbler you are, the better
The deeper the better
With deep humility, say to your family:

"Thank you for passing life to me
I am your descendant
I see all the countless pain and challenges that you have gone through
And I have seen how you have met with setbacks and failures
How you once cried out of loneliness
However, I thank you for being strong and tenacious
Fighting on for survival and life
Paying an incomparable price
Thank you
We have lived on till now
We have lived on till now
Your blood is flowing in my body
Your laughter, your sadness
Your dignity, your honor
All these are a part of me
I will bring this limitless wisdom and power
And create a better future
And help more people
To honor you

*Please give me your blessings
I will pass your blessings down on to the next generation
Thank you"*

(The person representing the family can now help you up)

*Then, stand up straight
And turn around
Let your family use their hands to support your back
Just like you have a huge mountain behind you
Unwavering, it continues to support you
Feel this power
Remember this power forever
Remember forever*

*Then, bring this power along with you
And face your future
Look at your future
And walk towards your future*

And happily give your future a big hug!

Chapter 7: Applying Principles of Relationships

The establishment of success and great exploits in life lies not in the knowing but in the doing.

-- Thomas Henry Huxley

The Deeper Mysteries of Relationships: Great Love Bringing To Completion

The Buddha once said, "All the phenomenon is born out of the Affinity." (萬法因緣生) (Chen & Lin, 2001).

In more than 20 years that I have spent helping people, I have come to a realization that: Life is not about solving problems but to bringing a completion to all the affinity we have with other people.

When we meet problems in life, if we look at it as a problem waiting to be solved, it would feel as if something bad has happened to us and so we need to "resolve it or get rid of it": But now that we have gone through so many words and real-life example stories, are you able to look at life from a different point of view? Do you have a deeper understanding about the deeper mysteries of relationships?

I have combined my experience of helping thousands of people through Constellations works together with Chinese traditional wisdom in order to come to a realization about this deeper mystery of relationships—"Great love brings us to a completion." (圓緣大爱), this means that relationships are a bridge used to complete the affinity we have with other people, a chance to learn great love for all in a more mature way filled with wisdom.

Completion of the great love does not require us to do things perfectly. We are not currying favor with anyone. We are not escaping from conflicts and trying not to cope with every lie. We are learning from each other. Through the completion of the predestined relationships we grow, we learn how to transform a love of desire into a love of wholeness.

Our children have got an affinity with us and that is why they are born into our family. When the child has some issues, are they the problem to be resolved? Our parents also have affinity with us and that is why we are born as their children. When there are problems between us and our parents, how do we complete this predestined relationship and make it whole? Our other half has an affinity with us, just like the famous Chinese saying, "As decreed by providence thousand miles of distance is nothing if you are to meet, otherwise you will never meet even if you are facing each other." (有緣千里來相會, 無緣見面不相識。) In the ocean of people out there in the world, two people actually coming together to meet each other is what we call affinity or fate. Even though our relationship may be filled with lots of pain and torment, but why did we meet each other in the first place?

All these affinities that have not been completed are like an incomplete circle, it becomes something we have not fulfilled in our hearts and eventually, all these unfinished businesses become a sort of 'gap' in our lives that tie our vital life force down. However, there is a deep motivation behind all these gaps. These gaps have all got a desire to be completed and filled up. If we are unable to complete it, out of the love for us, our children, or perhaps our grandchildren or one of our family members will try to help us fill it up. These become the entanglements that we pass on from generations to generations; or perhaps, let me explain it again using another concept we are more familiar with: If you believe in people being reborn into another lifetime, in order to complete the incomplete circle and fill in the gaps, we will become husbands and wives with these people or may become enemies so that we have another chance at completing all the affinity we have not been able to complete previously.

So how do we complete these affinities? When we have the affinity to be together, we have to learn to respect, learn to balance, learn to behave according to the order in our relationship, learnt to treasure; when the affinity has ended, we have to learn to say goodbye, learn gratitude, learn to let go and learn to how to bless them. Once we are able to apply all these Principles of Relationships that we have learnt, we will be able to grow love and wisdom in our lives and when we take action with love and wisdom, everything will definitely come to a full completion.

<u>U</u>**sing The Great Love to complete our affinity in our lives— this is the wisdom of love and it is also the very essence of Systemic Constellations.**

Starting To Apply Principles of Relationships

Through the deep realizations we have made previously, have you started to want to learn about Systemic Constellations? What about applying the Principles of Relationships?

Systemic Constellations is highly professional work. I do not recommend people to take it lightly and just follow suit on their own. The most ideal would actually for one to take part in some training and receive professional guidance. Currently, there are a few organizations and Systemic Constellations Facilitators conducting lessons all over the world. For more information, you could logon to the website, www.taos.com.tw or e-mail to us:systemicawakening@hotmail.com; should you have a problem that requires assistance, please work with a qualified Systemic Constellations Trainer or Facilitator.

For the most of us, we do not need to learn how to be doctors. The main point of our learning is to learn how to take good care of ourselves. We do not need to learn to be lawyers but we need to understand the basic norms of social interactions. Principles of Relationships mentioned here are basic principles governing the basic social interactions between humans. It is a Principle of Love and also the core concept of Systemic Constellations. All the exercises provided in each chapter are easy, practical and effective and are applicable anytime you like. Perhaps while you were reading this book, you would have already been aware of the disorder and imbalances within your own family; perhaps you may have been moved or inspired and want to readjust the way you interact with your family; or perhaps you have made some realizations and have already started to search for a change that will help you with your issue. In that case, taking part in a Systemic Constellations workshop will support you and help you get a better understand these Principles of Relationships and find a possibility to change.

For this purpose, I have come up with a "Family System Review Checklist" that will allow us to take a good look at our love and relationships. Please make good use of it and use it as a foundation for your observations and future actions.

Develop An Awareness For Your Love, Take Action Now

The following checklist will allow us to review the love within our family system so that we can apply Principles of Relationships to our lives and help us take the very first step to completing life's affinities for a better life. Please answer the following questions honestly. The more "No" answers you have, the more hidden entanglements you may have, the more the love within the family has unconsciously made you and your family members suffer. Should you like to improve your family relationships and let your love move in a better flow, should you want to clear up the entanglements and find your own position and your own power, Systemic Constellations will support you in accomplishing this goal.

Table For Reviewing Your Family Relationships

1. **Overall Sense of Belonging in Whole Family**

   - ♥ Do you know the names of your paternal and maternal grandfathers and grandmothers?
   - ♥ Do you know your paternal and maternal grandparent's personal histories and their characters and do you acknowledge and respect them?
   - ♥ When you talk about other family members at home, is your attitude one of respect?
   - ♥ Do you know who are included inside your family systems?
   - ♥ Do all the family members in your system have equal rights to belong to your family? Is there anyone who is being excluded?
   - ♥ Do all family members feel that they firmly belong to this family? Do the children feel a sense of belonging in this family?

- Do the people or children in your family who have passed away while they were very young have a place psychologically in your heart within the family?
- Towards the people who may have made mistakes, committed crimes or been involved in violence, does everyone in the family still see them as a part of the family?
- Do the husbands and wife give their aborted children a place in their heart and face the issue together?
- When facing with a crisis, does the family face it together?

2. **Returning To Your Position, Taking Up Your Own Responsibility**

- Are there any traditions that last longer than two generations in your family? Does everyone respect these traditions?
- Are the people who have been contributing long term to this family being respected? Have they been shown gratitude openly?
- Is the family aware what responsibilities the head of the family hold?
- Do parents feel that they are in service of this family and the people within?
- Does everyone work towards the harmony and happiness of this family?
- Are the roles, responsibilities and position of each and every family member clearly defined?
- Do the elders show an attitude of love and care for the younger ones in the family?
- Should the juniors need to be disciplined, are the elders in the family able to provide strict education?
- Do the juniors respect the elders? When they talk about their elders, are their attitudes positive?
- Are the junior able to express their disagreement with respect?

- ♥ When the husband and wife talk about each other, are their attitudes positive? Do they respect each other's parents and families?
- ♥ Do parents face up to their own conflict and disallow their children from interfering?

3. <u>**The Balance Between Giving And Receiving**</u>

- ♥ Does everyone feel that there is a balance between loving and being loved in this family?
- ♥ Does everyone appreciate the other family member's contribution towards them?
- ♥ Do you feel that your contribution towards the family and its returns are in balance?
- ♥ Are the family chores being assigned in a balanced way? Is everyone happy to accept the job scope that they are assigned to?
- ♥ Do the parents care about the needs of everyone in the family?
- ♥ If there is a crisis, are the elders willing to bear the responsibilities and risks involved?
- ♥ Do the husband and wife often openly express their gratitude and would like to repay the other person's contribution?
- ♥ Do the husband and wife feel that there is a balance between them? Is there an issue with their communication?
- ♥ Are the husband and wife happy about their sex life and do they feel a balance in the area of sex?
- ♥ Are the husband and wife able to express the hurt and negativity they feel and handle it with balance?
- ♥ Is the handling and interaction of money in the family reasonable? Is the disposition of the inheritance a smooth process?
- ♥ Are the monetary interactions between the family members and other people outside of the family smooth and successful? Does it also include inappropriate gains?

- ♥ Is there a common fund in the family to be used for the family's vacations, education and development?

4. **<u>Respect And Acknowledge The Truth As It Is</u>**

    - ♥ Is everybody's identity being acknowledged in the family?
    - ♥ Does everyone openly discuss the crisis happening in the family?
    - ♥ Is everyone in the family willing to admit their mistakes?
    - ♥ Does the family praise each other for good performances and acknowledges each other's success?
    - ♥ Towards the tragic deaths of the family, was everyone able to express their grief and accept the truth?
    - ♥ If one of the family has every killed or murdered someone else, or was being killed or murdered, have both parties come to a reconciliation in their hearts?
    - ♥ Can you respect your family secrets and be prepared to face it with respect?
    - ♥ Towards the people who have committed suicide, gone mad, become chronically ill or become addicted to something, does the family mention them with kind words and compassionate intent?
    - ♥ When talking about our parents or our own former partners, is the attitude friendly?
    - ♥ Is everyone aware of the financial situation in the family?

5. **<u>Living In The Present Moment, Moving With The Flow of Life</u>**

    - ♥ When you talk about the past, do you use terms of gratitude instead of complaining with negativity and grievance?
    - ♥ Are your family members able to keep themselves from repeating the same mistakes and learn from their past experiences/lessons?

- ♥ Are your family members able to let go of the past and continue to move forward?
- ♥ Do you feel that your parents would want you to lead a happy and successful life?
- ♥ When you are happy and successful, do you feel guilty towards your original family?
- ♥ When your original family and the family you started both need you at the same time, are you able to give priority to the family you started?
- ♥ Are the marriages in the family of all the adults in the family successful and smooth?
- ♥ Do your parents get along well with your spouse?
- ♥ Do you feel as if your parents have already given you the thing of the most precious?
- ♥ Do you pass on the love your parents have for you to your children?
- ♥ Are you living your mission of life and moving towards your goals and visions?

Transforming Into Actual Actions

If you can see clearly in the above checklist where your relationships, family systems or method of showing love have been in disorder, you can take action, starting from yourself. You can start by correcting the small deviations and you do not need anyone to help you. For example, if your parents quarrel with each other, you can remind yourself not to go against the Principle of Order. Do not intervene and remember to remind yourself to respect the way they handle their relationship; when you feel that your other half is good to you, remind yourself to really see him/her and return the favour with balance so as to let the Principle of Balance operate at its best; if your family tries to cover up or avoid talking about a family member who may have died young, contracted a chronic disease or contracted a mental illness, you will know that the Principle of Wholeness has been breached in the family. Therefore, you can explain the Principle of Wholeness to your family so that everyone can give this family member a place in their hearts.

In addition, there are also other positive and specific actions you can take. For example, start to bow down to your parents when you pay your respects to your parents during special days (For Chinese will do it in Chinese New Year). If you are already married, all the more you should bow down to the parents of your spouse during New Year and bring your child along when you do it. Let your child have a chance to learn how to respect their parents and be filial to his or her parents; pay respects to your deceased ancestors with a humble and respectful heart, commemorate a dead person at his grave during special days (For example, Chinese will do it during Qing Ming Festival); understand your grandparents and how they were as a person, thank them for passing their life on. Promise to make good use of this life and be even more successful and happy to help more people so that they can feel proud of you; start to make our family system chart, inquire about your family members and family histories from your elders. Bring the chart out during family gatherings, sincerely ask for help and discuss it with your family. Make a point to talk about those people who may have been forgotten or neglected. When you do that, the person who has been excluded or neglected would naturally return to their rightful place in the family in the hearts of all family members. Just by doing that, you will already be able to influence and adjust your family system.

If your family seems to have many major calamities and seem to have more entanglements; or you or your family members may be experiencing unexplainable emotions or repeating certain life patterns; or if you have lost all contact or information about your family; or if you have worked hard on your issue but it seems to not be improving, should you meet the above-mentioned situations, you can decide whether or not to conduct a Systemic Constellations for the issue. If the issue involves other members of the family, you may wish to discuss whether you would like to conduct a Systemic Constellations process for this issue. Should the answer be positive, please make sure that you seek help from a professional verified Family Constellations facilitator or trainer and work together with them to face the issue.

Ending: Awaken Your Inner Strengths

How do you love successfully? How do you bring an affinity to completion?

Only when we follow Principles of Relationships. This is because Principles of Relationships is the wisdom of love.

What are Principles of Relationships that we have talked about in this book? Let me summarize what we have discussed so far:

1. **Principle of Wholeness:** Respect the position of everyone in the system. Once again, see the people who were formerly excluded from the family system. Do not exclude them based on their actions or neglect them based on their fates. Even if husband and wife are separated, we do not deny each other's identity as parents. Learn to go beyond identifying with either the victim or perpetrator, move beyond the separation made by our minds, perceive that we are in fact a complete whole and are serving life together as a whole.

2. **Principle of Order:** Understand the systems we belong to and respect that there is sequential order between the elders and juniors in the family. When we love, we should do so from the correct order based on our position in the family. Respect our parents' fate and do not intervene with their relationship or conflicts. Repay our debt of gratitude towards our parents by leading happy and successful lives. Give priority to take care of our current family first, be accountable and take up our own responsibilities.

3. **Principle of Balance:** There has to be a flow of balance in the relationship between husband and wife. Return positivity with a little bit more, return negativity with a little bit less. The balance between child and parent would be to pass their life on to the next generation. Remember that inappropriate gains will bring about bigger losses, because other than material wealth, there are also intangible assets involved. In addition to a win-win situation, to give a little more. This will allow you

to create more wealth and harmony both for yourself and for others.

4. **Principle of Reality:** Respect and admit to the truth as it is in reality. This should be the foundation of all actions and behaviour; admit to and face up to all the unfinished businesses within the family and accept the tragedies that happened to the family; respect the reality and identity of every single person within the family system and do not deny the identity of parents to their children; if we live in the present and respect everything as it is, our love will be able to grow.

5. **Principle of Flow:** Live on and live on well. Life flows forward constantly, desperately holding on to the past would only put on our life on hold too. If we refuse to accept the past, it will create more entanglements in our life. How do we let the past become the past? Only through acknowledgement and gratitude will our past experience become our inner strength. All these sacrifices should not be in vain, we have to learn the lesson within and benefit from it. Link up with the source of life, and pass on our vital life force from one generation to another. Live our purpose and the future holds all sorts of possibilities for us!

Try to understand and experience these principles fully and deeply, they are the common result of the experience of many Systemic Constellations Facilitators. These principles have already helped many people and their families move their love towards the direction of success and happiness. You do not need to believe it but will need to experience it for yourself.

At the same time, please remember: these Principles of Relationships cannot be forced upon anyone. They are part of our innate nature; therefore, we need to be aware of it from within to apply and understand it from our daily lives. Only then can it become our true strength and our true wisdom.

Wherein lies the wisdom of love? Wherein lies Principles of Relationships? They exist within us, they are the principles within us. If there are no artificial barriers or human hindrance, our innate nature would naturally follow these principles of life and follow this greater power of ife because we have long been included into this greater power, we just need to realize that. So how does that feel? Let me share a tip with you. I guess you must have experienced this before. When you are doing something, you feel naturally focused on the present, you feel whole and fully integrated with it. Your body, your heart and your spirit is in sync as one, you forget your own existence, as if you are being encompassed and guided by a larger power—this is how it will feel when we follow the greater power of ife and it is also a movement in your inherent nature.

What does this mean then? It means that our innate nature is in fact joined and connected with the bigger power of life. Our internal nature is in fact moving together with great nature. We are all part of this great life. Anything that goes against the Principle of great nature will eventually fail. Therefore, if we can become nature and integrate with this larger power before use and bring our awareness into our love, these Principles of Relationships will naturally be applied to our daily lives. At this moment, we are love and love is us. This is what it means to be "moving with the Tao".

Lastly, I would like to share my poem with you:

Great love bring us to completion
Resonate yourself with natural principles
Moving with and melting into the great love
At this moment, we become
One.

Awaken the light within you and
bring awareness into your love,
Resonate it with the great love of the universe.
So we create a beautiful life together.
We are.

Exercise: Taking Action Within 48 Hours

Good, now is the new start of a new chapter of your life….

Please transform the wisdom of love you have learnt from this book into action. Do something loving either for yourself or your family that you can do immediately within the next 48 hours. Please be focused and write this action you wish to take down. Then, take actual action within the next 48 hours: Once we start to apply and follow Principles of Relationships to our lives, we will ignite the power of happiness and change our families, our lives and our world. We will create more harmony and happiness and create more wealth and love.

[Special Edition] By Other's Faults, Wise Men May Correct Their Own- Understanding Chinese Families

In the order of the family, the wife has her correct place "inside", and the man his correct place "outside" of the family. That man and woman occupy their correct places is considered the great righteousness shown by heaven and earth. In the family, we have an authoritative ruler; - that, namely, is represented by the parental authority. Let the father be indeed, father, and the son, son; let the elder brother be indeed, elder brother, and the younger brother, younger brother, let the husband be indeed husband, and the wife, wife: - then will the family be in its right state. Bring the family to that state and all the world will be established in harmony.
　　-- I Ching

家人，女正位乎內，男正位乎外。男女正，天地之大義也。家人有嚴君焉，父母之謂也。父父，子子，兄兄，弟弟，夫夫，婦婦，而家道正。正家，而天下定矣。
　　--易經

The special traditions and dynamics of Chinese families

To put things into context for readers from various cultures, I will like share a little more about Chinese families and highlight some common eastern and western cultural differences based on what I have noticed after facilitating Systemic Constellation sessions amongst Chinese families.

1) A Harmonious Family Is A Prosperous One

The phrase "a harmonious family is a prosperous one" (家和萬事興) is one every Chinese person will be familiar with. Loosely translated, it means that as long as a family is in harmony with each other, everything will fall into place and the family is certain to prosper. However, the unspoken implication behind this phrase is that for the sake of family harmony, many a times, Chinese people are being asked to suppress their emotions and bear with all humiliation for the greater good of the family. This results in superficial actions done in the name of harmony. In actual fact, these so called "harmonious acts" were merely attempts to help the family "survive" (Liu et al., 2011).

This characteristic of Chinese culture has greatly helped Chinese families survive in the past 5000 years. However, this trait also greatly reduces the value put on the uniqueness of each person, inhibits an individual's chance to shine and represses creativity. This is why someone once remarked that while China can easily reproduce thousands of iPhones, she will be likely unable to reproduce one person like Steve Jobs. (The founder of Apple's iPhones)

However, if we take a step forward and explore the deeper reasons Chinese people have for upholding this superficial harmony, we will discover that Chinese people have a strong sense of belonging to their families. To a Chinese person, one of the biggest punishments and humiliation one might experience would be to be chased out of one's own family. It is so important to a Chinese person that it may even trigger his or her fear for survival. Therefore, traits like showing high levels of loyalty to their families, suppressing their emotions for the family and lack of deep, meaningful communication between family members are much more common in Chinese families as compared to Western families.

2) Amongst All Virtues, Filial Piety Is The Most Important

"Amongst all virtues, filial piety is the most important" (百善孝為先) is common Chinese phrase. It means that amongst all the charitable acts one does and all the virtues one aspires to inculcate, the most important one and the starting point is "filial piety".

Sung (2006) pointed out that "Filial Piety" is a way to show love to Chinese parents. It is a type of love that respects and follows the order within the family. When we take a look at the words that the Chinese language uses to describe different types of love within the family, we will be able to see that this sort of love follows the order within the family.

In a Western family, the love between different family members will merely be described with a single word- "love". But in a Chinese family, the love a child has for their parents is called "filial piety" (孝順), the love a parent has for his or her child is called "affection" (慈愛) and the love between the elder sibling and the younger sibling is called "friendly love" (友善的愛), while the love that a younger siblings has for an older sibling is "respectful love" (恭敬的愛) (Liu et al., 2011). These different descriptive words show that the culture within Chinese families encompasses the concept of the "Orders of Love".

I suppose the focus on the "Orders of Love" is one of the main reasons why Systemic Constellation is very popular amongst Chinese people. In addition, Systemic Constellation also echoes what the great Chinese sage, Confucius, summarized about relationships two thousand years ago. Confucius called them the 5 cardinals of relationships: "Love to exist between parent and child, righteousness to exist between king and his ministers, differences to exist between man and wife, sequencing order to exist between elderly and child, trust to exist between friends." (父子有親，君臣有義，夫婦有別，長幼有序，朋友有信。) And he further emphasized that these are the fundamentals of life.

However, as most Chinese people do not have a complete understanding about the Orders of Love, a strength like filial piety eventually becomes a limitation instead. For example:

1. After marriage, many feel trapped between their original family and their new family. This is especially so for men. In order to uphold the important traditional thinking of filial piety, they will often list their parents as first priority and neglect their own families. This often results in common "in-law problems" between mothers-in-law and daughters-in-law. Should the husband's mother be unhappy about her daughter-in-law, should she share different opinions and be entangled in a hidden power struggle with the daughter-in-law, the husband and wife may even in extreme cases, even end up in divorce (Kung, 1999).

2. Because Chinese families put too much focus on the sequencing order within the family, this results in a lack of intimacy and a lack of freedom to show love. Chinese children born before the 70s rarely have any physical contact (eg, hugging) with their parents. In those days, you almost never hear the words "I love you" between parents and their children. This does not mean there is no love between them. It is just that they tend to show their love for each other silently through little acts of service Rarely do they show their love through words or physical touch. Therefore, it is easy for parent and child to have misunderstandings or to mistakenly think that the other party does not love them at all.

Liu, Li & Huang (2011) summarized that: To the Chinese, "filial piety" is the fundamental core of morality. However, many are trapped in "blind filial piety" (like blind love) and tend to sacrifice their happiness to show love and filial piety to their parents. Such examples are actually very common when we conduct Systemic Constellation for Chinese families. This is one of the biggest misunderstandings that Chinese people have today about "being filial". The most important book about filial piety in China, The Book Of Fillial Piety, (孝經) describes filial piety at the outset: "Our bodies, including our hair and skin, are given to us by our parents, so we must not presume to injure or destroy them. This is the beginning of filial piety." (身體髮膚，受

之父母，不可毀傷，孝之始也。)This means that the first thing you can do to show filial piety to your parents is to love yourself, love your body, mind and soul. Most Chinese people do not fully comprehend this and continue to blindly follow the unfortunate life patterns they see in their parents as a show of love and loyalty. This is what founder of Systemic Constellation, Bert Hellinger, calls "blind love".

So how do you make adjustments and manage both your original family and your current family nucleus? With the help what we have discussed so far about the huge emphasis on "order" and "filial piety" in Chinese families and the insights I have gained through observing thousands of Systemic Constellations done on Western families, many who have attended my workshops have found a way out— Firstly, one should learn to love oneself. After marriage, one should first take good care of our own family and when our parents become old, we can still take good care of them and show them filial piety, just like how they have loved us. If every generation were to do this, then we can leave a good heritage and the love can flow downwards through the generations smoothly.

3) Preference Of Sons Over Daughters

Preference of sons over daughters – a way of viewing sons as better than daughters, is a few-thousand-year-old concept in the Chinese family. Even though some countries in other parts of the world may share this preference, it is usually a little more extreme in Chinese families. When I was conducting workshops in various Chinese cities, this topic is a common and recurring theme. In many cases, the family will sell off their children due to extreme poverty and many times, baby girls are the ones who will be sold off while baby boys will be kept within the family. Some families will keep giving birth to more babies, just so that they can have a son in the family. I have also seen a few serious cases where the mother attempts to murder her daughter with her own hands by suffocating the baby, drowning the baby or even flushing the baby down the toilet bowl immediately after giving birth. All these are done out of their desire to have a son. For the sake of the important Chinese belief of continuing the family line through sons, countless of baby girls and their parents have paid a painful price. Hopefully, the Chinese society can self-reflect upon this belief and the actions it bring (Liu et al., 2011).

4) Adjustment Of The Imbalance In Marital Relationships

Favoring men over women is a concept that has also greatly affected Chinese marriages. There is a Chinese saying that goes, "A daughter who is married off is like water that has been thrown out." Even though modern Chinese marital relationships are moving towards equality, this thinking is still deeply rooted in the sub conscious minds of Chinese families.

For example, after one gets married, the wife is expected to be filial to her husband's parents and to be more filial to them then to her own parents. That is because in the Chinese mind, the wife is married "into" the husband's family and so as she is following her husband and belongs there now, his family takes precedence. She will naturally be required to also address his parents as "dad" and "mum" and to be filial to them. At the same time, when describing her in laws to others, she is required to use the terms "公公" and "婆婆" (which in this case means "father-in-law" and "mother-in-law" but these words can also literally be translated to mean 'grandfather" and "grandmother" too). She is required to address them in a similar fashion as her children (who are of lower 'rank' in the family). This way of addressing a woman's in laws has remained till this day and from this, we can see an obvious imbalance in the marital relationship between husband and wife. In addition, the wife's parents will actually ask their daughter to be filial to her husband's parents after she is married out of her family. On the other hand, the husband gets a wife who "marries into" the family. While he will also call his wife's parents "dad" and "mum", he is not required to be filial to his in laws and merely needs to show them some form of respect. To a man and his original family, they gain a "daughter" (媳婦- which literally translates to 'woman daughter') and so the "daughter" is required to be filial to her husband's parents. Therefore, a daughter that is married out of her family will lose a chance to show filial piety to her own parents as this job might be taken over by her sisters-in-law (the wives of her brothers). From this, we can see that Chinese families have a patriarchal family-oriented culture (Kung, 1999).

Like in many other parts of the world, if the husband and wife can find a way to live together in equality, the patriarchal family-oriented social structure can actually become even more valuable to our society. In Chinese culture, there is much emphasis on the "marital harmony" (夫唱婦隨- which literally translates to "when the husband sings, the wife follows" and 夫義婦從- which literally translates to "husband takes responsibility for his wife and the wife follows her husband"). But I notice that modern Chinese families usually only exemplify half of this saying. While husbands want their wives to follow them, they often forget to take responsibility for their wives. Or, the wives may want their husbands to be responsible for them but are unwilling to follow their husbands. This creates a lot marital problems for the family. Even though Bert Hellinger was born into and grew up in a western family, his insight echoes that of traditional Chinese wisdom. He says that "Women should follow their men and men should be in service to their women." Therefore, the crux of the matter lies in the "balance and equality" of a marital relationship. Finding out where this balance lies is not merely a challenge between husband and wife but a topic worth deep pondering over by all (Liu et al., 2011).

5) Ancestral Worship

Chinese families feel that even after a person passes on, they will still influence their future generations. We refer to this as "the blessings of our ancestors" (祖先庇佑) and "honoring of ancestral virtues" (祖德流芳). This is why Chinese families place a lot of importance on ancestral worship. Through the worship rituals, they are able to express their respect to their ancestors and remember them. During many festivals, Chinese families will prepare a lot of food and put them in front of the ancestral tablets, light some incense, and invite their ancestors to enjoy the food in their hearts. Through rituals like this, Chinese families also pray for their ancestors in hope that they will rest in peace, update their ancestors on what is happening within the family so that they need not worry, or ask for their blessings for the whole family to be bestowed with good health, a great career and family harmony (Sung, 2006).

Therefore, those who are familiar with Systemic Constellation will find that the ancestral worship rituals in Chinese families share many similarities and are actually a gentler form of the "reconciliation" process we often see Systemic Constellations.

However, within the Chinese family, there are often certain people who will be neglected or excluded. Some examples are: children who pass away when they were very young or divorced women. Children who pass away tend to be forgotten and divorced women are usually no longer included in the ancestral tablets in their husband's family even though they are also no longer included in the ancestral tablets in their own families too. If they do not have children, they will become "homeless souls" who will not be worshipped or remembered by any.

However, all these cannot stop love. As long as there is love within the family, even if there are children who have passed away or babies who died at birth or women who are divorced, love will prevail. Even if there is anyone who has been forgotten or excluded, should we give them a place in our hearts once again, love them once again, acknowledge them and respect them once again, and as long as husbands, wives and their family members learn how to find a balance that allows love to flow amongst each other, as long as everyone is given their place in the family and remembers their duties, the family then becomes a huge support system that empowers you to move towards completion and growth, while allowing each and everyone in the family to achieve their vision. This is why learning about Systemic Constellation is great help to each and every one of us.

Reference

A, N. I. (2017). *The Influence of Subconscious Mind on Human. Behavior.* Journal of Postgraduate Current Business Research, 2(2). Retrieved from http://abrn.asia/ojs/index.php/jpcbr/article/view/40

Chen, C. C. & Lin, D. J.(2001) *The Twelve Links in the Chain of. Interdependent Co-arising and the Relationships between the Universes of Buddhism and Science.* Buddhism and Science, Vol.2(1), 29 – 33.

Chun, M.I. (1998) *Post-traumatic Stress Disorder.* Airiti Library, Vol. 12(1), 3-8

Cohen, D. B. (2006). *Family constellations: An innovative systemic. phenomenological group process from Germany.* The Family Journal: Counseling and Therapy for Couples and Families, 14(3), 226-233.

Dasberg, H. (April, 2000). *Myths and taboos among Israeli first and. secondgeneration psychiatrists in regard to the Holocaust.* Echoes of the Holocaust (6). Retrieved June 9, 2005, from http://www.holocaustechoes.com/dasberg.html.

Drugge, U. (2008) *Family Trauma Through Generations: Incest and. Domestic Violence in Rural Sweden in the Nineteenth Century.* Journal of Family History, vol. 33, 4: pp. 411-429.

Essl, B. (2006). *Therapeutic application of family constellation work for. chronic illness.* International Constellations Journal, Vol. 7, 5-9.

Essl, B.(2008).*The healing dimension of grenzerfahrung in trauma. recovery.* Existenz: An International Journal in Philosophy, Religion, Politics, and the Arts,3(2),1-14.

Fang, T.W. & Shih, S.J. (2000) *Responses of Adolescents to Inter-Parental. Conflicts.* Guidance Journal, Vol.21, 93 – 134.

Franke-Gricksch, M. (2003) *You're One of Us: Systemic Insights and. Solutions for Teachers, Students and Parents.* Heidelberg, Germany: Carl Auer International.

Franke, U. (2003a). *The river never looks back: Historical and practical. foundations of Bert Hellinger's Family Constellations.* (K. Luebe, Trans.). Heidelberg, Germany: Carl-Auer-Systeme Verlag. (Original work published 2001)

Franke, U. (2003b). *In my mind's eye: Family constellations in individual. therapy and counseling*. Heidelberg, BW: Carl-Auer-Systeme Verlag.

Germine M.(1997) *The Concept of Collective Consciousness: Research. Perspectives*. The Journal of New Paradigm Research, Volume 48, Issue 1-4, 57-104. https://doi.org/10.1080/02604027.1997.9972608

Hellinger, B. , Weber, G. , & Beaumont, H. (1998). *Love's hidden. symmetry: What makes love work in relationships*. Phoenix, AZ: Zeig, Tucker & Co.

Hellinger, B. (2001a). *Love's own truths: Bonding and balancing in close. relationships* (M. Oberli-Turner & H. Beaumont, Trans.). Phoenix, AZ: Zeig, Tucker & Theisen. (Original work published 1994)

Hellinger, B. (2001b). *Supporting Love: How Love Works in Couple. Relationships*. Phoenix, AZ: Zeig Tucker & Theisen Inc.

Hellinger, B. (2003a). *Farewell: Family Constellations with descendants of. victims and perpetrators* (C. Beaumont, Trans.). Heidelberg, Germany: Carl-Auer-Systeme Verlag. (Original work published 1998)

Hellinger, B. (2003b). *Peace begins in the soul: Family Constellations in. the service of reconciliation* (C. Beaumont, Trans.). Heidelberg, Germany: Carl Auer-Systeme Verlag. (Original work published 2003)

Hellinger, B. (2003c). *Rachel weeping for her children: Family. Constellations in Israel*. Heidelberg, Germany: Carl-Auer-Systeme Verlag.

Hellinger, B. (2003d). *To the heart of the matter: Brief therapies* (C. Beaumont, Trans.). Heidelberg, Germany: Carl-Auer-Systeme Verlag. (Original work published 1999)

Horn, K. & Brick, R. (2005). *Invisible dynamics: Systemic constellations in organizations and in business*. Heidelberg, BW: Carl-Auer system.

Hsu, H. P.(2012) *The Operation and Coping Process of Yuanfen in Chinese Guanxi Interaction*. Indigenous Psychological Research in Chinese Societies, Vol.37, 57 – 97. DOI: 10.6254/2012.37.57

Hsu, Y. S., Su, W. N., & Hsu, Y. C. (2012) *Grief Responses and Adjustment Process of the Bereaved Siblings in Female Adulthood.*

Journal of Life-and-Death Studies, Vol. 13, 121 – 173. DOI: 10.29844/JLDS.201201.0004

Huang, C. C.(2003) *The Sinification of Buddhist Causation Theory.* Chung-Hwa Buddhist Journal, Vol.16, 254 – 282. DOI: 10.6986/CHBJ.200309.0254

Jiang, M. H. (2001) *The Subjectivity in Five Essential Relationships of. Confucian Ethics of Virtue.* Journal of National Hualien Teachers College, Vol. 13, 87 – 104.

Kung, H.M. (1999) *Intergenerational Interaction between Mothers- and. Daughters-in-law: A Qualitative Study.* Research in Applied Psychology, Vol.4, 57-96.

Lewin, K. (1947) *Frontiers in Group Dynamics: II. Channels of Group Life; Social Planning and Action Research.* Human Relations, vol. 1, 2: pp. 143-153. , First Published Nov 1, 1947. https://doi.org/10.1177/001872674700100201

Levine, P. A. (2005). *Healing trauma: Restoring the wisdom to your. body.* Louisville, CO: Sounds True.

Liu B.S.; Li, C.Y.; Yeh K.H. & Huang H.C. (2011) *Differences in Filial. Behavior in Multigeneration Families That Live Together.* The Journal of Nursing Research, Vol.19 (1) , 25-34.

Lin, C. N., Pan, H. P. & Huang, M. C. (2008) *Drawing up Pedigrees: Symbols and Meanings.* The Journal of Nursing, Vol. 55(1), 87 – 93. DOI: 10.6224/JN.55.1.87

Lin, H.Y. (2014) *Patterns of Interaction and Adolescent Problem. Behaviors: An Investigation of Maternal and Adolescent Perceptions.* Bulletin of Educational Psychology, Vol. 46(2),187-203.

Lin H.Y. (2015) *Parenting Practices, Stress Resistance and Adolescent. Problem Behavior: A Mediated Model.* Fu Jen Journal of Human Ecology, Vol. 21(2), 1-16.

Mahr, A. (1998). *Ein plädoyer für's innehalten: Systemische. familienaufstellungen bei Ttennung und scheidung [Systemic family constellations in separation and divorce].* In Gewagtes glück: Zu trennung und scheidung. Würzburg, Germany: Verlag Neues Buch Nidderau. Retrieved February 9, 2006, from http://www.therapie-im-wissenden-feld.de/literatur.html

Nelles, W. (2006). *Family constellation work: The method, the orders of. life, and the philosophical approach.* Journal of Life Studies, 1,

137-162.

Nichols, M. P., & Schwartz, R. C. (2001). *Family therapy: Concepts and. methods(5th ed.).* Boston: Allyn & Bacon.

Payne, J. L. (2005). *The healing of individuals, families, and nations: Trans-generational healing & Family Constellations.* Forres, Scotland: Findhorn Press.

Roy A. (2016) *Martin Buber and Rabindranath Tagore: A Meeting of Two. Great Minds.* Comparative Literature: East & West, 25:1, 30-42, DOI: 10.1080/25723618.2016.12015413

Schelotto, G. & Arcuri, C. (1986) *Supposing it hurt me too? Abortion: the. anguish experienced by men.* IPPF Eur Reg Inf. Spring 1986;15(1):25-34.

Sheldrake, R. (1995) *The presence of the past: Morphic resonance and. the habits of nature.* Rochester, VT: Park Street Press.

Shih, S.M. (2008) *New Concept of Grief Counseling-from Spiritual Growth. to Grief Transformation.* The Journal of Oncology Nursing, Vol.8(1), 27-33.

Sung, K.Y. (2006). *Reflecting on some questions of Chinese culture. through Hellinger's "Family Constellation".* Journal of Life Studies, 1, 163-168.

Tien, L. W. (2020) *A Case Report of a Depression-suicided Patient and. Family: Assessment and Intervention From Family System Theory.* Journal of Social work Practice and Research, Vol. 7, 65-89.

Ulsamer, B. (2005). The healing power of the past: A new approach to. healing family wounds. Nevada City, CA: Underwood.

von Bertalanffy, L. (1972). *The history and status of general systems. theory.* Academy of Management Journal, 15(4), 407-426.

Walsh, C. (2005). *The theory behind constellations.* Retrieved June 9, 2005, from http://www.constellationflow.com/constellation_theory.php

Zhang, B. H. & Hu, S. (2018) *Psychological Phenomena and Application. Values of the "Wide Angle" of Traditional Chinese Medicine: On Wholism in Traditional Chinese Medicine Psychology.* Research in Applied Psychology, Vol. 69, 3 – 22. DOI: 10.3966/156092512018120069002

Zhang, S. M., Ge, S. X. & Yang, Q. H. (2006) *Influence of Affects on. Cardiovascular and Cerebrovascular Diseases.* Chinese Journal of cardiovascular Rehabilitation Medicine, Vol. 15(1), 9 – 10.

[Appendix 1] TAOS Academy of Systemic Constellations

In 2001, Netra Chou (CHOU Tingwen) introduced Systemic Constellations to Asia and founded TAOS Academy of Systemic Constellations so as to provide a high-quality courses based on Systemic Constellations and also offering professional certification to Systemic Constellations work and its facilitators worldwide. He also started related workshops and trainings and published umpteen related books, hoping that this whole system view of self-help and helping others would support more people, families and enterprises to make good use of Systemic Constellations, helping them apply Principles of Relationships and move towards personal growth and personal awakening and nurturing. And all of these actions are in service of Life.

TAOS Academy (TAOS 國際系統排列學院)
www.taos.com.tw
+886-2-25783442 (Taiwan)
e-mail:systemicawakening@hotmail.com

[Appendix 2] Required Preparation Before Any Systemic Constellations Process

Before attending a Systemic Constellations workshop, please prepare the following information. The following questions apply to both you and your parents too:

- Did anyone in the family die young, pass away while they were a baby/child?
- When you were young, did any one of your parents pass away?
- Was there any of your family members being sent away or adopted? Are there any illegitimate children in the family?
- Are your parents the first intimate partner of each other? (Have they been married, engaged or have had intimate partners?)
- Has anyone ever had an abortion or a miscarriage?
- Family secrets (for example, a family member being excluded, uneven distribution of the inheritance, unlawful and inappropriate gains)
- Crime (for example, murder, being killed or causing of grievous harm)
- Does anyone in the family suffer from chronic disease, physical disability or addiction issues (for example, drugs, alcoholism or gambling)
- Did anyone in the family go crazy, commit suicide and become involved in acts of violence?
- Migrate

[Appendix 3] NETRA CHOU PUBLICATIONS

LOVE AND RECONCILIATION
LOVE AND RECONCILIATION is one of the best books introducing Family Constellations. It is also the first book to understand Chinese families and philosophy through Systemic work. The book contains 16 real-life examples of how Family Constellation is applied to create harmonious relationships and successful life. The book also includes several exercises designed by the author to help the readers apply what they have learned and benefit from it. It is a practical read for anyone keen to overcome challenges in their personal and or professional lives to enjoy better relationships, happiness, and success.

"I heartily recommend this book. I feel sure that it will assist its readers to resolve many riddles that stand in the way of a fulfilling life, both personally and in their professional success."
~ Bert Hellinger (Founder of Systemic Constellations)

BEYOND A CHILD'S MIND: a Deeper Understanding of The behaviours and Our Relationship
Every challenging behaviour of a child is a reflection of the underlying unsolved mysteries within the family from generation to generation.
This book focuses on exploring the deep psychology issue faced by our children and resolve using systemic constellation perspectives. Reconnect the missing links, develop more understanding love for our children so that they can develop their intrinsic motivation in life.

· Parents will realize their children's love and dedication to the family, and brave the stormy condition of growing up together with love and understanding.

· Educators will have a new perspective regarding the behaviours, and emotional changes of the children in providing diversify educational programs.

· Children's practitioners will explore more effective solutions to address the psychological factors behind the children's problems.

SYSTEMIC FAMILY CONSTELLATIONS: **Core Principles and Training Practices**

This book contains the introductory and key mentality to begin with, and step by step you will learn how to develop yourself to be a Systemic Constellation Facilitator. Including:
- What is Systemic Constellation and how does it work
- The Core knowledge, techniques, intuitive observation, and practical skills
- How to develop yourself as a Constellation Facilitator
- How to lead a Constellation workshop
- How to enhance the Power of Observation and Perception
- How to handle practices on-site in Critical Situations
- Four essential Steps to facilitate a Constellation
- Five laws of Life and relationships
- Eight working Models for common family issues
- Eight selected Case studies and Analyse the case with precision
- Nine Group Exercises in Systemic Constellation Work
- Top Ten Transformational Techniques

The content is very complete, practical, and unprecedented, and it is the most complete treasured training book in the field.

"We call this book 'Family Constellation Training Bible'."
~Mental Health Specialty Committee of Association for Life Care

HOLO-WISDOM: One-on-One Systemic Constellations and Online Constellations (in process of translating)